# Making Sense of Sensors

Implementing a Knowledge Pipeline

Omesh Tickoo
Ravi Iyer

Apress®

*Making Sense of Sensors*

Omesh Tickoo
Portland, Oregon, USA

Ravi Iyer
Portland, USA

ISBN-13 (pbk): 978-1-4302-6592-4
DOI 10.1007/978-1-4302-6593-1

ISBN-13 (electronic): 978-1-4302-6593-1

Managing Director: Welmoed Spahr
Lead Editor: Natalie Pao
Technical Reviewer: Waqar Malik
Editorial Board: Steve Anglin, Pramila Balan, Laura Berendson, Aaron Black, Louise Corrigan, Jonathan Gennick, Robert Hutchinson, Celestin Suresh John, Nikhil Karkal, James Markham, Susan McDermott, Matthew Moodie, Natalie Pao, Gwenan Spearing
Coordinating Editor: Jessica Vakili
Copy Editor: Kim Burton-Weisman
Compositor: SPi Global
Indexer: SPi Global
Artist: SPi Global

Distributed to the book trade worldwide by Springer Science+Business Media New York, 233 Spring Street, 6th Floor, New York, NY 10013. Phone 1-800-SPRINGER, fax (201) 348-4505, e-mail orders-ny@springer-sbm.com, or visit www.springeronline.com. Apress Media, LLC is a California LLC and the sole member (owner) is Springer Science + Business Media Finance Inc (SSBM Finance Inc). SSBM Finance Inc is a Delaware corporation.

For information on translations, please e-mail rights@apress.com, or visit www.apress.com.

Apress and friends of ED books may be purchased in bulk for academic, corporate, or promotional use. eBook versions and licenses are also available for most titles. For more information, reference our Special Bulk Sales–eBook Licensing web page at www.apress.com/bulk-sales.

Any source code or other supplementary materials referenced by the author in this text are available to readers at www.apress.com. For detailed information about how to locate your book's source code, go to www.apress.com/source-code/. Readers can also access source code at SpringerLink in the Supplementary Material section for each chapter.

Printed on acid-free paper

# Contents at a Glance

# Contents

# About the Authors

**Omesh Tickoo** is a research manager at Intel Labs. His team is currently active in the area of knowledge extraction from multi-modal sensor data centered around vision and speech. In his research career, Omesh has made contributions to computer systems evolution in areas such as wireless networks, platform partitioning and QoS, SoC architecture, virtualization, and machine learning. Omesh is also very active in fostering academic research, with contributions toward organizing conferences, academic project mentoring, and joint industry-academic research projects. He has authored more than 30 conference and journal papers and filed more than 15 patent applications. Omesh received his PhD from Rensselaer Polytechnic Institute in 2015.

**Ravi Iyer** is a Senior Principal Engineer, CTO, and Director in Intel's New Business Initiatives (NBI). He leads technology innovation/incubation efforts and has made significant contributions from low-power system-on-chip wearable/IOT devices to high performance multi-core server architectures including novel cores, innovative cache/memory hierarchies, QoS, accelerators, algorithms/workloads and performance/power analysis. Ravi has published over 150 papers, filed over 50 patents and actively participates in conferences and journals. Ravi is an IEEE Fellow.

# About the Technical Reviewer

**Waqar Malik** worked at Apple helping developers write Cocoa applications for the Mac during the early days of Mac OS X. Now he develops applications for iOS and OS X in Silicon Valley. He is the co-author of *Learn Objective-C* and *Learn Swift on the Mac,* both published by Apress.

# CHAPTER 1

■ ■ ■

# Introducing the Pipeline

The electronic world today is full of (a) sensors collecting data from various sources and (b) applications using this data for various uses. Our smart phones contain cameras, motion sensors, temperature sensors, microphones, GPS sensors, etc. Smart watches contain these sensors and more, like heart rate sensors, body temperature monitors, etc. The devices that we do not carry with us have sensors that monitor the environment, like the smart thermostats that can monitor if people are home for automatic temperature control, and cameras, including face detection for intrusion monitoring. While the world of sensors and associated sense-making seems to be getting crowded, intelligent, and highly complex, to understand the inner structure of this world one needs to know a few fundamental principles and flows. This book will use a few specific examples to illustrate these concepts in detail. In this chapter we present a high-level view and a taste of things to come later in this book.

## 1.1  Motivation

Readers who are curious about how the sensors collect environmental and behavioral information about us and how that information is processed to provide services useful for us will find the book helping them with concepts as well as pointers to build some of the basic solutions on their own. Understanding that all these complex services are built on similar fundamental principles is the foundational step toward this process.

As an example, consider a complex Advanced Driver Assistance System (ADAS) for automobiles (Figure 1-1). It uses a set of sensors like cameras, motion sensors, etc. to provide a driver with assistance for safety and comfort. One of the uses is to automatically track the position of a car in the traffic lanes and provide audible warnings in case the car drifts from its lane (Lane Departure Warning). This highly complex system works on the fundamental processing principles of Internet of Things (IoT) comprising of sensors collecting data (cameras, motion sensors), algorithms recognizing the data (relative position of the car in the lane, car drift), and applications acting on the recognized data (audible warning on/off). This flow shown in Figure 1-1 is the basic foundation for all the complex processing pipelines of sensor data as will become clear through various chapters in the book.

© Omesh Tickoo and Ravi Iyer 2017
O. Tickoo and R. Iyer, *Making Sense of Sensors*, DOI 10.1007/978-1-4302-6593-1_1

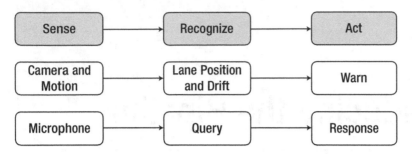

***Figure 1-1.*** *Stages in sensor data processing and applications*

As another example consider the automatic voice-based personal assistance provided by the smartphones and other devices. In such usages, a user activates the system with a voice command and then asks a query like, "*What is the weather going to be like tomorrow?*" The system "*magically*" understands the question and provides a verbal answer to the query. At the heart of this complex system is the now-familiar (sense, recognize, act) methodology. The microphone senses our speech, the recognition system "understands" our intention and the action is taken to satisfy the request.

The following chapters in this book aim to provide the readers with a high-level view of the steps it takes to process data collected by various sensors for it to be useful for various applications. We will understand the logical steps needed to convert data to knowledge and deep-dive into some specific implementations that will make it easy for the readers to "*play*" with the code and data to understand the details of the implementation.

At a very high level, the data captured from the physical world goes through the three stages shown in Figure 1-2 in order to become actionable knowledge.

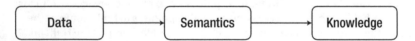

***Figure 1-2.*** *Data lifecycle stages*

The first stage shows the data captured by various sensing devices (video, audio, pressure, motion, temperature, etc.). The data is raw (unprocessed) and combined with noise of various types and needs to be cleaned, filtered, and represented in a structured manner in order to be useful for analysis and processing. Assume, for the present discussion, that all these processing steps are represented by the data block in the Figure 1-2.

The data by itself is a series of single measurements at specific periods in time. To understand what the data is actually "*telling,*" an observer needs to extract the semantics in the data. For example, while an ambient temperature reading of 100° F by itself tells us the absolute temperature sampled by a thermal sensor, its semantics are not immediately understood. Coupling this information with the fact (assumed) that the measurement was taken near a glacier in Alaska in winter with previous measurements gradually increasing in magnitude gives us a contextual and semantic understanding that something unusual is happening at the location of measurement.

Understanding the semantics embedded in the data allows us to grasp the significance of data in context. In addition, the semantic relationship to other facts understood so far can be understood. These relationships form the basis of *"knowledge."* As a very simplistic example, in the instance of the temperature reading above, a correlation with another event like a major forest fire can provide the understanding for the underlying cause of the anomalous temperature reading.

One of the facts embedded in the example discussion above is that *"knowledge feeds on itself,"* i.e., the system can know that the high temperatures in Alaska are an anomaly if it already *"knows"* that typically the weather in Alaska is cooler. So we can redraw the Figure 1-2 as shown in Figure 1-3 with a feedback loop in the knowledge builder.

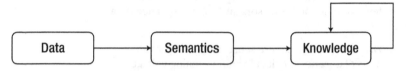

**Figure 1-3.** *Iterative knowledge model*

Knowledge refers to an aggregate of the semantic information extracted from the sensor data arranged in a manner that the relationships are extended over the entire knowledge base through links that build over time as more and more semantic information is available. There are two main structural parts to the knowledge management task:

1.  **Knowledge representation:** Knowledge needs to be stored and represented in a manner such that the semantic information and relationships between various concepts is retained and is modifiable. The modifications to the knowledge include addition of new information and entities, including changes in the current relationships or representations catalyzed by new data.

2.  **Knowledge operations:** These include tools, APIs, and programming languages to insert and extract data from the knowledge database. Knowledge storage needs to provide means to insert a new relationship at the correct place in the existing knowledge database. This involves understanding the incoming semantic data and providing a mechanism to find and manipulate the correct relationships. The extraction process involves responding to different queries targeting relationships between different entities and concepts. The input to the extractor is an incomplete relationship description and the output fills in the gaps in the description. The extractor needs to support a logical language that can mathematically represent queries like, *"What wine should I order with grilled chicken and restaurant X?"* and provide a mechanism to walk the knowledge database to obtain the answer.

## 1.2    Next Level of Data Abstractions

Now that we are familiar with a high-level description of the functional blocks, we present a brief overview of the data abstractions in an end-to-end pipe. The abstractions show how the data collected from the physical world through sensors transitions to ultimately generate usable and actionable information.

For the purposes of this book, we are concerned with the following sub-levels of data abstractions.

1.  **Raw Sensor Data:** Raw (or unprocessed) sensor data is captured by sensors at the front end of the pipeline. The format of the data varies with the type of the sensor. Below are a few examples of the sensors and their associated data formats:

    a.  *Vision:* Typically, camera sensors take still or video shots of a scene. The data format is analog voltage levels representing pixel intensities and color at various locations on the image sensor. These levels are frequently sampled and quantized to bits, making the signal easier to manipulate digitally. This process is called analog-to-digital conversion.

    b.  *Audio/Speech:* The microphone-like sensors typically capture the audio and, if the goal is to transmit the information over a network or process them through digital tools, a process called analog-to-digital conversion is applied to achieve the conversion, and the result is a stream of bits representing audio frequencies over time.

    c.  *Motion:* Inertial sensors typically measure the acceleration and motion (transitional and angular). The data produced is a stream of numbers representing the instantaneous change in the parameters described above.

    d.  *Temperature sen*sors generally report the instantaneous temperature at a certain instant in time.

    e.  *BMI sensors:* The Brain Machine Interface sensors, like EEG and EKG, report the brain activity measurements as activity graphs. Figure 1-4 shows a commercial BMI sensor that can be worn on the head like headphones.

***Figure 1-4.*** *BMI sensors*

2.  **Features:** Generally speaking, we are interested in the certain higher-level information in the data that in its aggregate can lead to recognition of target entities. As an example, locating edges or corners in an image can be a first step toward recognizing discernable objects. Similarly, identifying micro-utterances in an audio stream enables stitching of them to create words.

3.  **Recognized entities:** Recognition is generally a complex task involving spatial and temporal analysis of the extracted features to map the aggregate to pre-known entities. Continuing with the examples above, in case of vision, the recognition task may involve classifying the extracted features to recognize shapes like objects and faces. For audio, statistical analysis and classification of features allows for aggregated features to be recognized as words. Typically, the tools for recognition are pre-trained with examples of entities that they eventually "search" for in the feature pool. A face recognition algorithm, for example, will be trained for specific faces with multiple images of each face used for training. Once trained, the model can identify the trained faces from the test images.

4.  **Semantic relationships:** Semantic relationship extraction, along with contextual relationship extraction, has become increasingly important, especially as machines become more intelligent in understanding the environment around them. Semantic relationships refer to the connection between various recognized entities. For example, the semantic relationship between a key and a lock refers to the operation

of opening or closing the lock with the key. Similarly, the sentence *"I like coffee"* connects "I" (the subject) with "coffee" (object) using the predicate "like." Many simpler semantic relationships can be represented by such (subject, predicate, object) triplets. Figure 1-5 graphically shows the relationship triplets with an example.

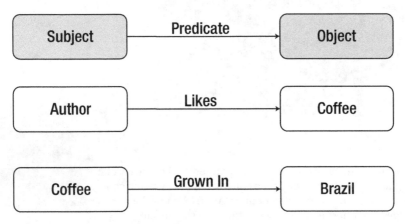

***Figure 1-5.*** *Semantic relationships*

5. **Contextual relationships:** Contextual relationships help understand the recognized data in context. The context can be obtained in multiple ways. These include using other sensors as well as using the history of recognized data for context recognition. A face recognition operation that was performed by a surveillance system can identify a potential invasion or normal operation depending on when the recognition took place (day vs. night) or depending on the person that was recognized.

6. **Knowledge:** One way to look at the concept of knowledge is to visualize it as a bigger aggregate of relationships connected together through predicates. Addition of more and more relationships results in a graphical knowledge structure that has a directed relationship between nodes representing the predicates. For example, the semantic relationships *"I like coffee"* and *"coffee is grown in Brazil"* results in a compound knowledge entity as shown in Figure 1-6.

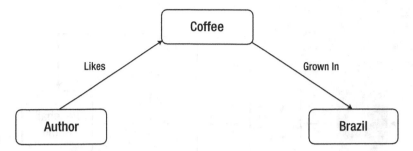

***Figure 1-6.*** *Basic knowledge building block*

Extending this concept leads to a rich knowledge base, examples of which can be found as part of a semantic web. One such database is shown in Figure 1-7, representing relationships between food types. The representation could, for example, be used to interpret that fruits can be sweet or non-sweet and in either type are edible.

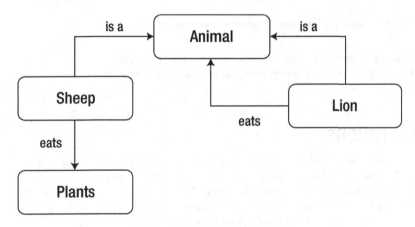

***Figure 1-7.*** *Extended relationship graphs*

7. **Query and Response:** The knowledge base is ultimately intended for providing information in order to implement services for various usages. Various forms for data analysis algorithms operate on the knowledge nodes and relationships to extract information useful to provide the services desired. The query process focuses on constructing a semantic search input to the system that results in the analytical algorithms parsing the knowledge base for an appropriate response. For example, using Figure 1-8, the query "What is the flavor of shellfish?" can be resolved and an answer (moderate or strong) can be provided as the response.

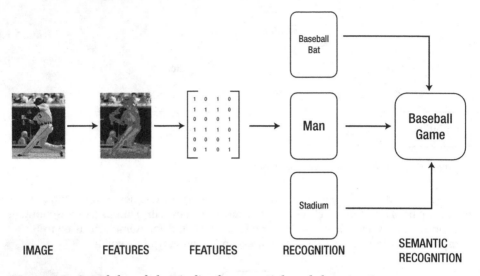

**IMAGE**     **FEATURES**     **FEATURES**     **RECOGNITION**     SEMANTIC RECOGNITION

***Figure 1-8.*** *Sample knowledge pipeline for semantic knowledge extraction*

Figure 1-8 summarizes the discussion so far in an example knowledge pipeline showing an image recognition pipeline in various stages.

# 1.3   Operations

As we move in the knowledge and analytics pipeline from the raw sensor data acquisition to usage implementations, each data transformation is brought about by specific operations performed on the data generated by the previous stages. While the nature of transformation operations varies by the nature of the data, the goal of analysis, and available resources, we can broadly categorize the operations under abstractions given below:

1. Feature Extractors: Raw sensor data to Features

2. Recognition Algorithms

3. Multimodal context extractors

4. Knowledge Extractors

5. Knowledge Representation Frameworks

6. First order logic operations

7. Analytics

Keeping these operations in mind, Figure 1-8 can now be shown with the transformation operations as shown in Figure 1-9.

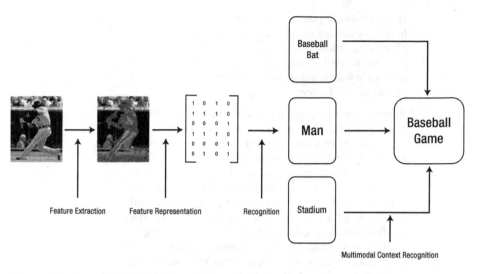

*Figure 1-9.* *Figure 1-8 with data transformations*

We now present a brief description of each of these transformation operations.

1. **Feature extractors:** The primary job of feature extractors is to obtain the first level of "*interesting*" information from the raw data collected by the sensors. The goal of the feature extraction operation is to *reduce the data size to be processed.* Sensors produce a lot of data, much of which contains redundant and "uninteresting" information for an application under consideration. Processing this unneeded data through the whole pipe will amount to wasted compute resources, higher processing latencies, wastage of power, and bandwidth overload. Extracting features early in the pipeline ensures we separate the needed information from the rest of the data and reduce waste.

   *Also,* having features compatible with the processing goals of the rest of the pipe enables the subsequent stages to be designed easily with optimal functionality for operating on the data that is known to have relevant information. In the absence of feature extractors, the subsequent stages would have to implement complex operations to "*search*" through the entire data for relevant information to use.

   Depending on the type of data and the goal of analysis, the feature extractor implementations vary. For example, in a visual understanding system that is trying to recognize faces, a feature extractor could implement skin-based segmentation schemes that allow it to only send data with skin color information to the other stages. Similarly, another vision system implementing object recognition could have a feature extractor implementing edge extractors that provide object edge information to the recognition module. In audio analysis, instead of sending the raw audio to the analytical engines, a feature extractor implementing frequency extraction can be used.

2. **Recognition:** A recognition module implements algorithms to detect and label entities from the features provided to it. Typically a recognition algorithm is trained to identify certain entities by feeding it examples of true and false results. This phase, commonly known as "*training the model,*" leads to parameters of the algorithm being configured in such a manner that it acts as a filter to output a certain result when one of the trained entities is recognized. A trained model usually needs to be retrained for recognizing new entities. Exceptions exist in some limited cases where the model can be self-learning or self-training. Examples of recognition algorithms include the now immensely popular Convolutional Neural Networks, Bayesian and non-Bayesian classifiers, and temporal filters for recognizing events in time. Implementations of these algorithms can determine if a visual feature set embeds a face or an object, what word was spoken, and what action one is performing based on sensors used and the features extracted.

3. **Multimodal Context Extractors:** Recognized information from one or more sensors can be combined to understand the operational "context" of the knowledge pipe. The context extraction process uses the available recognized outputs to provide an understanding of the environment in which the events are occurring. Having access to such information can be crucial to the proper usage implementation.

# 1.4　Constraints and Parameters

The discussion so far focused on the logical partitioning of the data types and data understanding algorithms through various steps in the knowledge generation pipeline. In addition, there is another level of operations partitioning that a designer or an architect will need to consider while designing such a pipeline. The partitioning is the direct result of mapping the abstract pipeline above to the real physical pipe. Depending on the usage, the implementation of the components described above will be constrained by the parameters shown in Figure 1-10. These parameters also serve as a design input for the implementation to determine how to partition the functional blocks discussed so far between different hardware platforms available end-to-end.

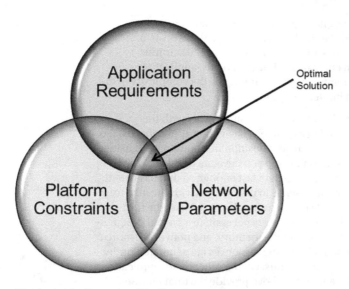

**Figure 1-10.** *Execution Pipeline Constraints*

1. **Application performance requirements:** Each application operates under certain performance requirements. Some applications need to run real-time, which means that the results need to be provided by the application with an acceptable time constraint so that a user feels the interaction with the application is happening in a natural fashion. This is similar to how one would get responses from a human who we are interacting with face-to-face. Other applications need a predefined level of results accuracy. Some applications can live with approximate results while others need a precision that can, in turn, mean higher computation requirements.

    a. *Accuracy:* Assume an application (AppA) is interested in determining how many people enter a building during a given day. Contrast this with another application (AppB) that wants to know exactly *"who"* was entering the building. AppA implementation needs us to distinguish a human from anything that is not human (pets, machines, etc.) while monitoring the building entry points. A human classifier at the recognition stage in the pipeline does not have to be a very complex algorithm and can be implemented by approximating many of the computations. As long as we can reliably distinguish humans from others, we need not implement algorithm blocks that calculate the exact height, posture, and gender of the people. Contrasting this with AppB, we can imagine that the relevant recognition algorithm

11

is very complex, since it is trying to analyze various facial features and then comparing these to an existing database of known faces to accurately determine a person entering the building. Thus, application requirements can greatly influence the complexity of the solution implementation.

b. *Latency:* The latency requirements vary with the application. For example, a navigation application that is predicting your current position in a building and using that information to help you navigate to a destination needs to analyze the data fast enough so that it is useful. It does not make sense to provide you with the next turn information if you have already moved past the turn. Such real-time constraints necessitate a system design that considers compute, memory, and network resource allocations such that the responses are generated under tight latency constraints. On the other hand, applications like AppA and AppB above provide the total number of people or the actual faces that entered a building as a list at the end of the day and may not have tight latency constraints (although, if used for security purposes, the applications may have tight latency constraints as well). They can collect the data from the relevant cameras and work on the data offline to generate the results. Knowing the latency constraints of the applications under consideration allows the system designer to make necessary implementation trade-offs.

2. **Power Constraints:** Each platform on the end-to-end pipe operates under some form of power constraint. The available power for the sensors and sensor nodes collecting raw data is usually limited and they are battery-operated. In contrast, the nodes in the last stage of the pipe tend to be wall-powered servers with large power budgets. Ideally, one would like to execute all the "*heavy*" work portions of the pipeline on the platforms that are rich in computation resources and power. This would mean executing on servers (or the "cloud," as the server "back end" is commonly called) for most implementations. But combining the power constraints with the other constraints, especially the application constraints as discussed above, underlines the need for running at least some functionality at the front end and other intermediate stages of the pipeline.

3. **Network constraints:** Generally, the network infrastructure will be shared among various different applications and available network resources change dynamically over time. Network constraints mainly consist of the following:

a. *Bandwidth:* The total amount of bandwidth available directly affects the throughput of the applications. Based on the available capacity and the other applications competing for the network bandwidth, the time it takes to transfer content over the network for the application will vary. A pipeline designer typically tries to reduce the amount of total bandwidth requirement to keep the application performance optimal and predictable. This might entail trying to run more parts of the application close to the data source (a goal opposite to that dictated by the power constraints) and transmitting smaller size processed information instead of unprocessed data (e.g., transmit features instead of raw data).

b. *Reliability:* Different network protocols provide applications with different levels of service. A reliable transport, for example, will provide guaranteed delivery of all the data but the latency might be higher in case some data is lost over the network and retransmissions become necessary. On the other hand, an unreliable protocol can trade off fast transmissions with an occasional loss of data packets. The designer needs to carefully choose the best possible network protocol based on application needs.

4. **Memory Constraints:** Each platform on the pipeline has limited memory. For an operation to execute on a platform, the processor needs the data it operates on to be resident in the memory. In case of the memory size being too small when compared to the amount of data/code needed by the processor to effectively process the application, the platform runtime infrastructure will need to manage the movement of resources (code/data) to and from the memory. This operation introduces latency in processing in addition to introducing power overheads. The memory constraints usually tend to push the parts of the pipe that need more memory toward the back end of the pipe where the execution can take advantage of servers.

5. **Resource sharing constraints:** At each stage in the pipe, the physical resources like processing, power, memory, network, etc. are generally shared between different applications. Having shared resources makes it very complicated for the designers to build architectures for predefined performance. There exist schemes to guarantee a minimum level of performance and share of resources (Quality of Service) to help out in these situations, but these schemes generally come with a cost. We will discuss more about these in the

coming chapters. Figure 1-11 shows the transition of resource availability as we move from front-end sensors to back-end servers. In the figure, LOW and HIGH refer to the resource availability (Bandwidth, Power, and Memory) or computation characteristics (Accuracy expected).

| | | |
|---|---|---|
| Bandwidth | HIGH | LOW |
| Power | LOW | HIGH |
| Memory | LOW | HIGH |
| Accuracy | LOW | HIGH |
| Response | FAST | SLOW |

| Sensor Node | Gateway | Server |
|---|---|---|

**Figure 1-11.** *Balancing the constraints*

In summary, a system designer has to efficiently map the end-to-end capability blocks to available hardware under the performance constraints as described above. The resource manager in Figure 1-12 needs to find the "sweet spot" of execution based on all the constraints mentioned above.

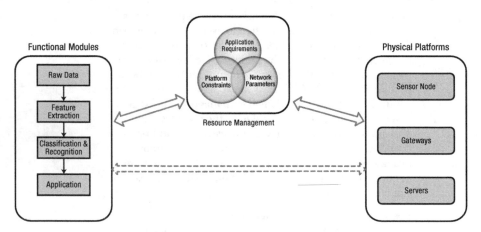

**Figure 1-12.** *Designing the system under constraints*

# 1.5    Physical Platforms

Our final section in this chapter presents a quick summary of the physical platforms used to execute the functions of the pipe.

**Sensors/Smart Sensors:** At the front end of the pipe are the sensors that collect the data. These include cameras, microphones, gyroscopes, accelerometers, thermometers, altimeters, air quality sensors, and many more. Some sensors can be smart in the sense that they are able to process some of the data on the node itself. The processing could result in smarter transmission policies to save battery or some initial processing; or trigger some action on the sensor nodes based on the nature of the data captured.

**Gateway/Router:** The gateways and routers comprise the intermediate platforms in the pipeline. They serve two very important roles in the end-to-end pipeline.

a.   Routers and gateways serve as intermediate platforms with more compute resources than the sensor nodes but are much closer in terms of network distances than high-powered servers. This property makes it possible for many applications to take advantage of the compute proximity of these intermediate platforms for low-latency and low-overhead functions executions.

b.   These intermediate notes act as aggregation points for data being transmitted from various sensors. In addition to being the relaying point for the collected data to the cloud-based servers, these platforms are the first in the pipeline to have the ability to cross-correlate data from multiple sources. If resources permit, the intermediate platforms can work with data from multiple sources to determine context and reduce data redundancies before transmission to the servers. The routers and gateways also keep track of the nodes connected to them and transmit, configuration, and node management commands needed.

**Cloud/Server:** The servers comprise what is known as the back end of the pipe. The back end is also referred to as the "cloud." The cloud is generally well-equipped with high-capacity wall-powered servers capable of high-compute cycles, as well as large memory banks. The cloud is the appropriate place for heavy computation. The disadvantage of executing workloads at the cloud have to do with network-introduced latency. Real-time applications may not be able to tolerate the delays in getting responses over the network from servers. So servers are generally suited for offline batch processing like analytics. Knowledge representation and query/response processing on knowledge databases are some of the typical functions carried out on the servers.

## 1.6   Summary

In this chapter we introduced a high-level overview of the process to convert data collected by the sensors into actionable information through recognition. We touched upon how data transforms through the recognition pipeline and different operations performed on the data. We also talked about practical considerations to implement such processing pipelines on real physical systems. Chapter 2 will dig deeper into these operations with specific examples.

## 1.7   References

- World Wide Web (W3C) Consortium, Semantic Web Standards
  (https://www.w3.org/standards/semanticweb/)

- Institute for Human and Machine Coordination
  (https://www.ihmc.us/)

# CHAPTER 2

■ ■ ■

# From Data to Recognition

The process of recognition in the digital world begins with sensors that capture raw data about the physical world. In this section, we will focus on three types of sensors (inertial, audio, and visual) to understand how these are used and how data from these types of sensors can be recognized for different purposes. Let's start by considering a few different usage scenarios in mobile, wearable, and IoT deployments. Mobile Devices: Today's mobile devices have many sensors to understand user context and behavior, and enable personalized interaction. Figure 2-1 shows a few example sensors in mobile devices and the type of data they provide. Inertial sensors enable understanding the movement of the phone along different axes including acceleration, rotation, etc. Audio sensors enable the phone to hear sounds such as a question from the user. Visual sensors enable the phone to capture pictures and videos that may provide a better understand of location or objects in the vicinity.

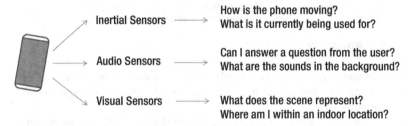

**Inertial Sensors** ⟶ How is the phone moving?
What is it currently being used for?

**Audio Sensors** ⟶ Can I answer a question from the user?
What are the sounds in the background?

**Visual Sensors** ⟶ What does the scene represent?
Where am I within an indoor location?

***Figure 2-1.*** *Example sensor usage from mobile phones*

It should also be noted that the combination of these sensors can provide multi-modal recognition, providing even richer contextual data. For example, combining audio and visual sensors can provide a better understand of the activity in the scene. Using a visual sensor, one can see a kid and adult in a scene that may indicate an adult teaching a child. Adding audio sensing to the context gives additional information that the activity is singing as opposed to talking for example.

Wearable Devices: Much like mobile devices, wearable devices also employ similar sensors but now have the ability to determine the user's movement and audio/visual focus and interaction, potentially from a first-person perspective (e.g., head-worn devices). Figure 2-2 shows types of usages that such wearable sensors can be used for.

O. Tickoo and R. Iyer, *Making Sense of Sensors*, DOI 10.1007/978-1-4302-6593-1_2

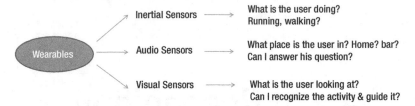

**Figure 2-2.** *Example sensor usage from wearables*

IoT devices: While similar sensors may be used in IoT devices, a key difference with IoT devices is that they are typically looking at a scene and a collective rather than focused on personalized scenarios from a user point of view. As an example, IP cameras are used for monitoring residences (homes) as well as road intersections and traffic. Here, the cameras are generally static or move in limited range, so the use of audio/visual sensors is the focus instead of the inertial sensors. The visual sensors provide the ability to understand scene changes, as well as identify the number of cars or people in the vicinity. The audio sensors add additional information by providing information such as significant anomalies in sound (like an accident on the road or a window break-in in the home). Figure 2-3 illustrates this usage.

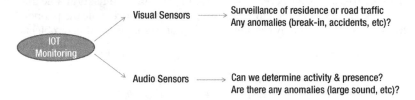

**Figure 2-3.** *Example sensor usage for IoT*

Again, the use of multi-modal (audio + visual) recognition also helps significantly in these cases, since we can correlate accidents and home break-ins using both sounds and visual clues simultaneously.

The rest of this chapter is organized as follows. We will start by looking at the sensor types in more detail and then go into depth on the recognition techniques for each of these sensor modalities and associated usages.

# 2.1   Sensor Types and Levels of Recognition

As mentioned above, there are multiple types of sensors, ranging from inertial to proximity/location to audio/visual. In this section, we will introduce three such sensors (inertial, audio and visual) and describe how they generally work.

## 2.1.1   Inertial measurement unit

The accelerometer is the best place to start understanding inertial measurements. An accelerometer essentially measures the force (proper acceleration) along each axis. Typically, such devices are referred to as 3-axis accelerometer since they provide force along x, y and z-axes. A gyroscope helps determine orientation by measuring rotation across a given axis. Figure 2-4 provides an illustration of the accelerometer and gyroscope data capture. The two together can provide acceleration and orientation and may be referred to as a 6-axis sensor. Depending on the usage model, data from these sensors are typically captured at rates ranging from few Hz to KHz. Raw data from an accelerometer/gyroscope is typically noisy and the use of filters is common to ensure that these are smoothened based on multiple data points. Such sensors can be applied for a wide variety of use cases, examples below:

- Understanding of position/orientation helps mobile phones today re-orient the screen in portrait or landscape mode and reverse direction as required.

- These sensors also enable simple gestures to be recognized based on buffering continuous data and looking at the change in force and orientation. These gestures could be as simple as "shake" vs. "roll" vs. a "circle" motion along a certain axis.

- Sensors are also used for navigation purposes but are relational since they provide force in a given direction but do not provide absolute location in any field. Typically, this approach is known as dead reckoning and requires other sensor information to ensure that there is not a significant drift caused over time in the relative positioning due to the noisy sensor data.

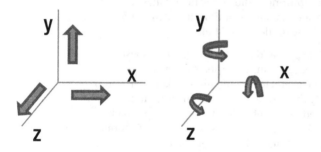

*Figure 2-4.* *Intro to accelerometer, gyroscope and IMU*

## 2.1.2   Audio Sensors

The typical audio sensor used in most devices is a standard microphone. Microphones convert sound to electrical signals and are prevalent in many applications ranging from the typical public addressing systems to movies to laptops to mobile, wearable, and IoT devices. In this section, we primarily focus on the microphones used in lower-end devices for IoT and wearable applications. Most of the microphones used in these devices are

MEMS (microelectromechanical systems) sensors and are likely to be analog or digital. The output of the microphone is typically pulse-density modulated (PDM) or pulse code modulated (PCM) and data is captured from 4-bit to 64-bit and can be tuned for signal-to-noise ratio and quality of the capture. The typical frequency response of microphones range from 20Hz to 20KHz. To improve the quality of the recording and recognition, sometimes two or three microphones are used in mobile phones, for example. This allows for processing the data from each of these microphones and reducing the noise to deliver higher quality output (e.g. voice clarity when making a phone call).

Audio sensors are used for not only capturing and recording content, but also for audio classification and speech recognition (see Figure 2-5). Here are some of the predominant usage scenarios for single or multiple microphones in mobile, wearable, and IoT systems:

- Audio classification: A common IoT use case for microphones is to classify the environment that the sound was captured in. For example, capturing audio every so often from a microphone in a kitchen can provide information on what type of activity is currently going on—idle, dishwashing, water running in the sink, cooking, etc. Researchers are using machine listening techniques such as this to go as far as to disambiguate the different noises in the background. For example, audio captured from a phone could provide information about not only the foreground human voice but also what is happening in the background.

- Voice Activity detection: Another common use case is voice activity detection. Here the focus is on attempting to determine whether there is voice in the captured audio. This is helpful when a phone or other device is completely off except for the microphone that is capturing audio at low rates. Once there is voice activity in the audio, then the audio subsystem is powered on and more processing (as described below) is done.

- Speaker recognition: Speaker recognition, sometimes also referred to as voice recognition, attempts to determine who is speaking. This can be useful to identify the speaker in an audio transcript or identify the speaker as part of an authentication approach. When used as part of an authentication approach, it is important to differentiate between speaker identification (identifying one amongst multiple speakers) and speaker verification (determining that a specific speaker whose signature has been captured before was the one who spoke).

- Keyword recognition: Keyword recognition is probably the simplest form of speech recognition where the focus is to ensure whether a particular word was uttered. Keyword recognition can be speaker-dependent (trained for a particular speaker) or speaker-independent (generally applicable for all). Keyword recognition can also be generalized to keyphrase recognition and both are typically used as triggers for additional activity such as starting a session of commands or bringing up an application.

- Command and Control: Command and control refers to using a small set of phrases in speech recognition. For illustration, this could include a set of commands to control a toy car such as "move forward," "move backward," "go faster," "go slower," "turn right/left," etc.

- Large vocabulary continuous speech recognition (LVCSR): LVCSR and CSR in general refer to the continuous recognition of speech as it is fed into the speech recognition system. This typically involves a moderate to large vocabulary that is recognized. Of all of the above, this is the most challenging and computationally complex speech recognition problem and there have been a number of advances in this area recently enabling reduced error rates and better general usage.

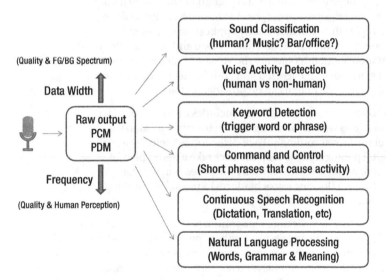

**Figure 2-5.** *Audio sensors and recognition capability examples*

Building on the above techniques, applications that are more interesting and capabilities that may be of potential interest to the reader are natural language processing and language translation capabilities. These capabilities are now emerging in different market solutions.

## 2.1.3   Visual Sensors

The most common visual sensor is the camera. Cameras are well understood since they have been around for ages for photographic purposes. In this book, we focus on their use as a visual sensor to recognize what a device can automatically see, understand and act upon.

Unlike inertial and audio data, visual data introduces a spatial dimension to the data, since it can be 2D or 3D in nature. A camera can be used for instantaneous 2D capture (still image) without any temporal information, or as part of a video capture with rich temporal data capturing multiple frames over time. Generally, data can be captured at extremely low fidelity (e.g., QVGA that is 320x240 as a still image or at few frames per second) to high fidelity (e.g. HD and 4K at 30 or more frames per second). The capture rate depends on the usage model that needs to consider whether human consumption (as in replay) is the key requirement or whether only machine recognition of some visual aspect is sufficient.

Visual recognition can be used for many different purposes ranging from object recognition, face recognition and scene recognition to similarity/anomaly detection, understanding motion or scale, and video summarization. Some examples of these are provided in Figure 2-6 and are listed below for illustration:

- Object Recognition: Object recognition refers to the basic idea of identifying objects in an image and potentially matching them to a pre-existing database of objects that have been captured before. For example, an augmented reality application can identify a monument or tourist attraction in an image and provide additional information about this object to the viewer. Similarly, an object in a retail store can be recognized and additional information about health, price, and content can be provided to the user.

- Face recognition: Face recognition includes detection of a face in an image as well as matching that face against a database to label the face accordingly. Face detection is useful by itself for digital photography to help the user take a better picture. Face recognition is useful for many purposes ranging from authentication (logging into a platform) to social networking applications (such as Facebook).

- Gesture recognition: Gesture recognition refers to the recognition of static poses or moving gestures either specific to the hand/arm or the human body. Recent game consoles commonly use examples of these where a player uses his hands and entire body to interact with the game. Static poses are easier than dynamic gestures since it generally involves processing a still image and matching it against a pre-existing set of captured still gestures. Gesture recognition can also be user-dependent or user-independent, where the former requires the system to be trained for a specific user whereas the later builds in enough modeling to accommodate for any arbitrary user.

- Scene recognition: Scene recognition is extremely complex and an ongoing research problem. The simplest form of scene recognition is to take an entire scene and match it against known ones. A moderate form of scene recognition involves identifying multiple objects, faces, and people in an image and using that information to determine the likely activity or context. The more complex form of scene recognition requires the system to differentiate two scenes accurately despite similar objects being in the same two scenes.

- Similarity/Anomaly Detection: Anomaly detection is a common challenge in visual recognition especially in scenarios where cameras are used for surveillance, including home monitoring as well as traffic monitoring. Here, the key is to identify if any anomaly occurred which should trigger additional analysis. Such solutions focus on identifying a set of known signatures statically or dynamically and thereby determining if any significant changes in the frame have occurred since.

- Video Summarization: Video summarization is a meta application that can use many of the above techniques in order to summarize the salient aspects of a long video stream. This includes scene changes, key scenarios and objects/characters that are the focus of the video. Video summarization enables the user to jump to specific parts of a video or quickly identify which video is being looked for amongst a set of existing videos.

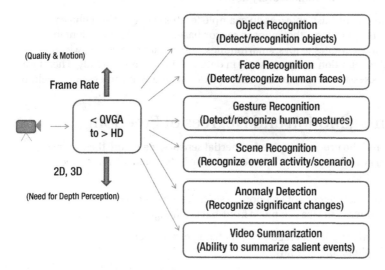

**Figure 2-6.** *Visual sensors and usages*

It should also be noted that the inertial, audio, and video sensors and recognition techniques can be used in conjunction for multi-modal recognition. In the descriptions below, we will start by studying the recognition techniques for each independently and then show examples of combining them together.

# 2.2   Inertial Sensor Processing

This section presents a brief overview of how sensors are used to measure device motion and inclination. As mentioned earlier, the inertial sensors can also be used to recognize certain gestures. We focus on inertial sensors. Specifically, the goal is to provide a high-level functional overview of MEMS (Micro-Electro-Mechanical Systems). We will not be diving into the details of the construction of these sensing systems but will focus on the data understanding part.

Device motion can be measured through two fundamental ways:

Measuring motion through external device observation: Cameras outside a device can observe and map the device behavior.

- Pros: Very useful in controlled environments to measure movements of somewhat generic objects

- Cons: Can only work in defined areas, dependent on lightening, etc.

Measuring motion through internal device instrumentation: This involves instrumenting the device with onboard sensors that measure the motion from the device itself.

- Pros: Can measure fine motion and tilts almost universally

- Cons: Need to instrument every device

We will use the second case above as an example for this section. This choice was made for two main reasons. First, the onboard sensor-based method is prevalent in devices ranging from wearables to toys, smartphones, and airplanes. Second, we are covering the visual recognition and processing in detail in this chapter already. Therefore, we will dedicate this session to introduce a new type of sensor and its processing pipeline.

## 2.2.1   Defining Motion and Degrees of Freedom

Before we understand the processing pipe for inertial sensors, we define the Degrees-Of-Freedom (DOF) available to a device. We define 6 such degrees as enumerated in following two categories:

- Translational Degrees of Freedom: 3 such degrees of freedom exist, namely a device can move front-back, left-right or up-down.

- Rotational Degrees of Freedom: 3 such degrees of freedom exist, namely pitch, roll, and yaw.

Figure 2-4 shows the degrees of freedom in a pictorial fashion.

An Inertial Measurement Unit (IMU) consists of the following two common devices to measure the motion:

Accelerometer: An accelerometer is a device that is "supposed" to measure acceleration. In practice, the device reacts to inertial force. Main uses for the inertial sensor are to measure translational acceleration and inclination with respect to the earth "plane."

Gyroscope: A gyroscope is mainly used to measure the motion along an axis. This includes the pitch, roll, and yaw motions in Figure 2-4. The motion is measured as a "rate of change" of the angle along an axis.

Typically, to interface the IMUs with the rest of the device system, an Analog-to-Digital Converter (ADC) is used that converts the generated voltage to a bit pattern (number). This number gives a measure of motion or inclination (along one or more axes). Figure 2-7 shows a simplistic view of the IMU processing pipe.

**Figure 2-7.** *Recognizing IMU data*

## 2.2.1.1   Accelerometer

An accelerometer detects the force in the opposite direction from the actual acceleration vector. This force is also described as the *fictitious force* or *inertial force*. The only place where an accelerometer will not experience any measured force is in space of while going through a free fall. Thus, it is important to have a measure of "resting force" or the "resting measurement" from the accelerometer. This force equals the force of gravity that is being experience by the device at all times. Typically, each measure of the force will need to adjust for gravity in order to extract the actual acceleration of the device relative to its position on earth.

We will demonstrate the working of an accelerometer by concentrating on a single axis accelerometer device. Assume that the accelerometer measures force along the z-axis. An analog accelerometer measures the inertial force as a shift in the voltage output by the device. Typically, to interface the accelerometers with the rest of the device system, an Analog-to-Digital Converter (ADC) is used that converts the generated voltage to a bit pattern (number). This number gives a measure of inertial force in a given direction (along an axis). The following definitions come in handy to understand the accelerometer behavior:

Reference Voltage/ADC reading: This is the measure of resting force as described above. The constant gravitational force can result in measurements on a different axis based on the IMU and device orientation, as we will find out shortly. Material and design defects can also contribute a non-zero value to the resting reading of such devices. We need to compensate for this measurement when we use the accelerometer for any real world usages.

Sensitivity: The sensitivity of the accelerometer refers to the change in voltage (or ADC output) per unit of acceleration measured. Many systems use the acceleration due to gravitational force (g) as the unit of acceleration. Thus, the sensitivity can be measured in volts/g.

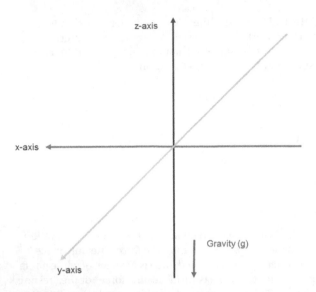

**Figure 2-8.** *Accelerometer linear acceleration measurement axis*

Given the definitions above, the Figure 2-9 shows the process of calculating acceleration along a single axis. For simplicity, we assume the vertical axis as the axis of measurement so that the gravitational force acts on the same axis and can be accounted for by a simple subtraction. We shall soon see how to deal with a more general case.

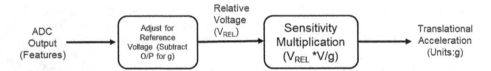

**Figure 2-9.** *Single axis accelerometer operation*

Multi-axis Accelerometers: In case of accelerometers with multiple axis measurement capability, the device can measure acceleration along each of the defined axes. For example, a 3-axis accelerometer can measure inertial force/acceleration along the x, y, and z axes. It is important to note that any acceleration measured by the device is reported in the form of its x, y, and z components as shown in the Figure 2-10. In Figure 2-10 the direction and magnitude of force (acceleration) is denoted by the vector D. Accelerometer outputs will report the magnitudes components in x, y, and z direction denoted by the projections Dx, Dy, and Dz, respectively. To get an accurate measure of the magnitude and direction of the acceleration, one needs to know the orientation of the axis as defined by the manufacturer. Fortunately, one other property of multi-axis accelerometers comes to our rescue in such situations.

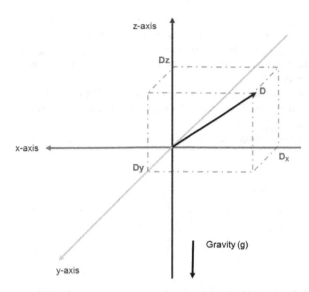

**Figure 2-10.** *3-Axis accelerometer operation*

Measuring inclination: The fact that multi-axis accelerometers measure gravitational force at rest can be used to calibrate the accelerometer. At rest, the accelerometer measures the inclination of the device with respect to the ground. With an axis perfectly aligned in the vertical direction, the other two components of the measured voltage (or ADC values) will be zero. Thus, aligning the device in multiple positions and taking the ADC readings from these positions can pinpoint the exact orientation of the accelerometer axes.

## 2.2.1.2   Gyroscope

Accelerometers measure the translational acceleration (up-down, right-left, front-back). There are 3 more degrees of freedom a device can have in its movement. These relate to angular motion. Specifically, these are termed as pitch, yaw, and roll. These are shown in the Figure 2-4. A gyroscope measures the angular motion in terms of degrees-per-second about the x, y, and z axes. In gyroscope speak, we refer to the measure of each degree of freedom as a channel. Thus, a 3-channel gyroscope can measure all of the 3 components of angular motion (pitch, roll, and yaw).

Similar to the accelerometer discussion above, the Gyroscope outputs are analog voltages converted to ADC digital outputs. The voltage changes are linearly related to the rate of change of angle around a given axis. After processing the ADC output, the gyroscope readings are generally reported in degrees/second around specific axis. Similar to the accelerometer discussion we define the following:

Reference Voltage: The gyroscope reference voltage refers to the ADC "step size." In simplest terms, it defines the amount of voltage it takes to increase the ADC output by one unit.

27

Zero Rate Voltage: In the case of a gyroscope, this voltage is measure of inherent bias in the device. Ideally, a device at rest should report a reading of zero on all the gyroscope channels. However, the material and design defects lead to a non-zero resting reading on almost all such devices. This reading should be subtracted from the measurements to get the right angular motion measurements.

Sensitivity: The sensitivity of the gyroscope refers to the change in voltage (or ADC output) per unit of angle changes measured. The gyroscope sensitivity can be measured in millivolts per degree per second.

In line with the accelerometer processing, the gyroscope sensor-processing pipeline is shown in the Figure 2-11.

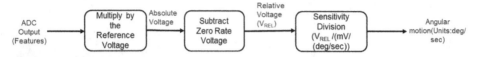

***Figure 2-11.*** *Gyroscope processing*

### 2.2.1.3    Combining the accelerometer and gyroscope readings

To get the accurate measurement of device inclination and motion for all 6 DOF, we combine the readings from the accelerometer and the gyroscope. The main complication in getting to the motion and inclination estimate from various ADC readings is to confirm the orientation of the IMU axis. Usually the manufacturer provides this information as part of IMU datasheets. However, the placement of IMUs in various devices can differ, and a user needs to calibrate the device before making sense of the ADC measurements for accelerometer and gyroscope. Usually the calibration step involves moving the device about various orientations (vertical, horizontal) and using the resulting readings in linear projection equations to solve for axis orientations.

### 2.2.1.4    Gesture Recognition Using IMU

Combined accelerometer and gyroscope readings from a device can be used to recognize specific device gestures. For example, a phone equipped with an IMU can recognize a circular gesture through the IMU. This gesture can then be linked to different actions, like making specific sounds turning the camera ON, etc. Many modern smartphones use the IMU to allow a user to flip a phone face down for declining a call or stopping music playback. Modern toy manufacturers are building robotic toys that use inertial sensors to plan motion and in conjunction with other sensors like cameras, to react to human interactions. There will be more on multi-sensor integration in the next chapter.

# 2.3  Audio Processing and Recognition—From sound to speech

As described in the previous section, recognition using audio sensors (i.e., microphones) is growing in popularity as more phone/wearable/IoT devices start to implement these to capture good quality audio data. In this section, we will go into a bit of depth in audio recognition is accomplished from audio classification to large vocabulary speech recognition. To start with, a simple pipeline of audio and speech processing stages is illustrated in Figure 2-12.

***Figure 2-12.*** *Stages of audio/speech recognition*

Let's walk through each of these stages and examine the audio recognition techniques used. Before we do that, it should be noted that the first step in processing audio for recognition is to process the audio signals and extract key features. The most common features extracted from audio are known as MFCCs (Mel frequency cepstral coefficient). There are many different ways in which MFCCs or variants thereof can be computed. The Mel frequency cepstrum (MFC) represents the power spectrum of the sound and the coefficients (MFCCs) are calculated by first taking windows of the audio sample, taking the Fourier transform, computing the power spectrum, mapping on to the mel bin, computing the log of the energy, and performing a discrete cosine transform to determine the amplitudes. More details on MFCCs can be found in the literature (such as one by K. Prahlad et. al. in references).

## 2.3.1  Audio Classification

We start with audio classification (see Figure 2-13) which is typically focused on non-human sound and attempts to understand and label the sounds captured. The traditional approach for audio classification is to identify key features such as MFCCs that may help separate the sounds into different classes and then use machine learning techniques to train/classify them. More recent techniques have attempted to add additional features specific to audio classification that help improve the accuracy. Some of these techniques may be content-specific, but there are others that are more generic, such as the addition of temporal fluctuations and roughness/loudness/sharpness as described in the "Features for audio classification" by Breebart et al. in references. Once the feature set is determined, standard machine learning classification techniques can be used. Standard classification techniques include nearest neighbor algorithms, Bayesian algorithms, Gaussian mixture model (GMM) and others. More recently, neural networks are used to enable supervised and unsupervised approaches to audio classification.

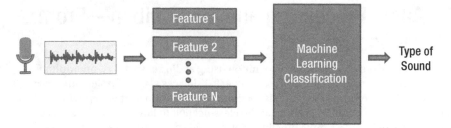

**Figure 2-13.** *Audio classification example*

## 2.3.2    Voice Activity Detection

Voice activity detection (VAD) refers to the detection of human sound in the audio capture. Figure 2-14 illustrates the general VAD processing flow. VAD is typically used as a trigger to move into the next phase of speech recognition such as keyword or command/control. There are several different types of VAD implementations in the literature and commercial solutions. Examples include the use of simple filters, such as recognizing pitch, to more sophisticated approaches that use GMM (Gaussian mixture model), statistical models and energy-based VADs. One of the key challenges in VAD is the level of noise in the audio capture. As a result, noise reduction and cancellation techniques typically go hand-in-hand with VAD solutions. In Man-Wai Mak et al. from references, the authors show that noise reduction and elimination of background signals are key to improving accuracy of VAD solutions. Ultimately, the voice activity detector can be used for reducing the amount of processing that needs to be done for speech recognition since it acts like a filter. As a result, it is important to optimize the solution to reduce false negatives (indication of lack of human voice when it is present) as opposed to false positives (indication of human voice where is there is none).

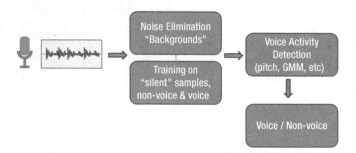

**Figure 2-14.** *Voice activity detection example*

## 2.3.3    Automatic Speech Recognition (ASR)

Automatic speech recognition or ASR refers to the ability for a computer system to recognize human speech and convert it into text. ASR comprises of capabilities ranging from keyword recognition (KR), command and control (CC), and large vocabulary continuous speech recognition (LVCSR). KR is typically used as a trigger to wake up a system whereas CC as well as LVCSR is used as part of a session to either control an activity or do dictation of a text passage for email or other purposes. While keyword recognition can be implemented in a more custom manner, the general techniques for KR, CC, and LVCSR can be similar with the differences largely in the size of the vocabulary and grammar comprehension. Figure 2-15 shows the general speech recognition processing flow. Speech recognition can be implemented to be speaker-independent, where any speaker can interact with the system, or speaker-dependent where the system trains based on a specific user or set of users. Common speech recognizers or toolkits that are used for learning and exploration include CMU Sphinx (`http://cmusphinx.sourceforge.net/`) and Kaldi (`http://kaldi-asr.org/`). Customized versions for specific targets such as mobile devices include PocketSphinx (`http://www.speech.cs.cmu.edu/pocketsphinx/`).

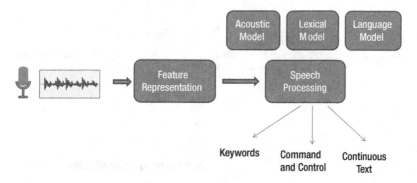

***Figure 2-15.*** *Automatic speech recognition*

Traditional approaches to speech recognition are based on the use of GMMs (Gaussian Mixture Models) and HMMs (Hidden Markov Models). The key problem being solved is to figure out the most likely sequence of words based on the incoming sequence of acoustic observations. For example, the initial implementations of speech recognition employed the following key processing phases:

- Feature Extraction: The incoming speech signal is broken into frames of 10ms each. Each 10ms sample is represented by a feature vector that comprises of 39 components.

- GMM scoring: To determine the senones in the speech and identify the best match, GMM scoring is performed on the feature vectors provided.

- HMM processing: The model of the speech requires HMM processing to determine the most likely sequence of sounds and words based on the provided vocabulary (lexical models and language models).

Until recently, most (LVCSR) speech recognizers were based on the GMM+HMM approach. However, the performance of speech recognizers was not adequate to achieve mass adoption at high quality. Performance metrics for speech recognizer include word error rate, speed and overall accuracy. In order to address these, recent speech recognizers started exploring the use of weighted finite state transducers (WFST) and deep learning (neural network) for speech recognition.

Neural networks are growing in importance for both speech and vision processing. Deep neural networks are essentially artificial neural networks with many hidden layers between the input and the output layer. DNNs replace the use of GMMs in speech recognition flow (see Figure 2-16), moving it from GMM+HMM to DNN+HMM solutions. Most commercial offerings in speech recognition these days are based on deep neural networks because it improves the word error rate and overall accuracy of the system.

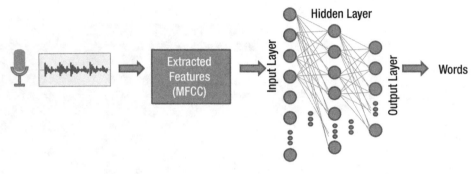

*Figure 2-16.* *Using deep neural networks in ASR*

Weighted Finite State Transducers are used to represent HMMs but provide additional information that could speed up the processing, since each edge in the directed graph is labeled with inputs, outputs, and weights. As a result, WFST is a rich mathematical framework that has uses beyond HMMs in natural language processing as well.

## 2.3.4    Natural Language Processing (NLP)

NLP involves taking text from speech-to-text solutions or written text and trying to extract information or gain deeper understanding of the text in an automated fashion. The first step in NLP is to understand tokenize the text by understanding sentence construction and identifying word boundaries. Another important step is to use named entity recognition (NER) to categorize specific words into more general classes where appropriate. Figure 2-17 shows an example basic flow of NLP. During this process, individual words can also be assigned weights in relation to the type of NLP analysis being accomplished.

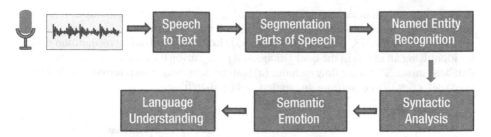

**Figure 2-17.** *Natural Language Processing example*

Once these initial processing phases are completed, machine learning techniques are applied to analyze the key aspects of text. For example, the emotion of the text (positive, negative, etc.) can be determined by analyzing the words in the text. The topic of the text can be identified by classifying the words in the text with the most likely topic association. The nature of the question asked in the text can also be determined for usage models such as what Siri and Cortana are targeted at.

In the above section, we introduce the key aspects of audio/speech recognition, ranging from audio classification to voice activity detection to automatic speech recognition to natural language processing. We hope the overview of each of these areas provides an understanding of the key usages, the key components or algorithms used, and the considerations when developing such techniques. While we did not go into depth into the algorithms themselves, the reader should be able to identify which algorithms need further examination depending on the usage model of interest and the focus of the exercise.

# 2.4 Visual Processing and Recognition

The visual recognition starts with a basic camera sensor that can capture both still images as well as video. Visual recognition, as described earlier, can include object recognition, gesture recognition, face recognition, scene recognition, anomaly detection and video summarization. In general, visual recognition follows the following basic process: feature extraction, descriptor generation and matching. Features are extracted from the image, and then they are summarized as a descriptor vector, following which they are compared against a pre-existing database of vectors for the recognition of interest. We will describe this process with some examples for each of the recognition categories stated above.

## 2.4.1 Object Recognition

Object recognition refers to the ability to detect and recognize objects in an image or video. Examples of object recognition range from identifying a cereal box or bottle of wine in an image to identifying a historic monument in a tourist spot. The overall usage may be counting the number of items on a retail shelf (cereal boxes or wine) or providing more information (augmenting the reality) to the tourist pointing the phone camera at a monument. While we will describe the typical flow of object recognition below from a single object point of view, note that the same applies for identifying multiple objects with clustering and bounding techniques included for this purpose.

Figure 2-18 (from S. Lee et al. in references) shows a typical object recognition flow for identifying an object in the query image and recognizing it by matching against a database image. The basic flow includes (a) feature detection (also referred to as interest point detection), (b) descriptor generation and (c) matching.

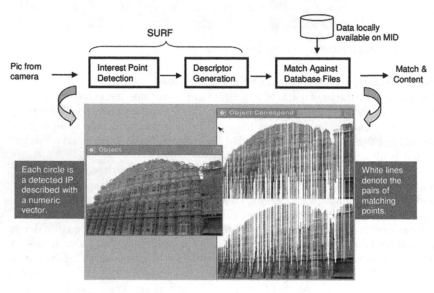

***Figure 2-18.*** *Object recognition flow example (S. Lee et al.)*

Many algorithms have been developed and optimized over the years for object recognition. These include SURF (speed up robust features) (reference by H. Bay et al.), SIFT (scale invariant feature transform, reference by D. G. Lowe et al.), ORB (reference by E. Rublee et al.), FAST (reference by E. Rosten et al.), BRIEF (reference by M. Calonder et al.), and BRISK (reference by S. Leutenegger et al.), to name a few. These algorithms provide the ability to identify feature points in the image that uniquely describe the object(s) and then descriptor generation approaches to describe the region surrounding the feature point as part of a descriptor vector. Initially, algorithms were designed for basic functionality and accuracy. However, with the ubiquity of mobile devices integrating cameras, these algorithms optimized for reduced computation complexity, increased speed, scale invariance, rotation invariance and noise resistance. The reader is referred to each of the papers for the algorithms to understand the specifics of the algorithms better. For illustrative purposes, an example flow is shown in Figure 2-19.

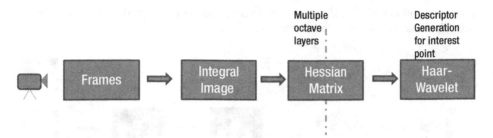

*Figure 2-19. Object recognition flow (e.g., SURF components [references by S. lee et al., H. Bay et al.])*

Once the features/descriptors are determined, the next step is to match it to recognize the object. A matching database holds previously captured descriptor vectors, and matching the query descriptor vectors to the database provides the ability to get the nearest match or set of matches as the output. Typically, this match is done by either brute force (l1, L2 distance calculations) as shown in Figure 2-20. In addition to brute-force, ANN (approximate nearest neighbor) approaches are also very common, especially as the size of the database increases significantly. There are fast libraries for ANN computations, such as FLANN (`http://www.cs.ubc.ca/research/flann/`), that are commonly used for performing these computations at maximum speed and efficiency.

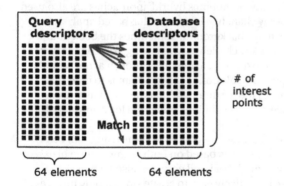

*Figure 2-20. Brute-force match using L1/L2 distance calculations (S. Lee et. al.)*

## 2.4.2   Gesture Recognition

Gesture recognition refers to the ability to identify and recognize hand poses, dynamic hand gestures or similarly body poses or dynamic body actions. Gestures have recently become more popularized by the Kinect (`http://www.xbox.com/en-US/xbox-one/accessories/kinect`) as it is used commonly in game consoles like the Microsoft® Xbox (`http://www.xbox.com/en-US/`). Figure 2-21 shows the steps in identifying hand pose and facial features using skin color-based segmentation. In this section, we will start with the basic hand pose recognition for describing the process. The simplest form of hand pose recognition is to identify whether there is a hand in the image (detection) and then identify the specific hand pose (recognition).

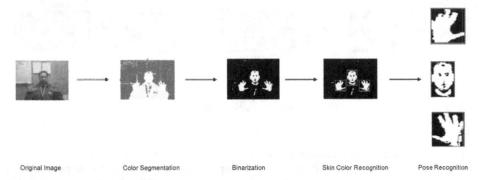

Original Image        Color Segmentation        Binarization        Skin Color Recognition        Pose Recognition

***Figure 2-21.***  *Gesture recognition examples*

Hand detection is typically accomplished using two different types of mechanisms: (a) skin color of the hand and (b) model describing the typical hand shape. There are many algorithms that look at the different colors in the image and try to identify whether there is a hand in the image and thereby segment that part of the image to do more processing for recognition. Color spaces that are usually employed when doing skin color analysis includes RGB, HSV, YUV and YCrCv. Sometimes hybrid approaches are also used considering multiple color spaces. The key challenge in doing color-based analysis for hand identification is the nature of the image background. Sometimes the background color may be similar to skin color. Another key challenge when using skin color is that human skin color varies from person to person. So making the approach agnostic to the user is also somewhat challenging. A possible solution to this problem is to make the solution user-dependent, but that imposes the requirement that the user has to train the system through an enrollment process. Most solutions prefer the least amount of enrollment/user training required.

Figure 2-22 shows an example of the hand segmentation scheme using skin color analysis. As shown in the figure, the final answer is based on both segmentation of the skin and then comparison to a known model of hand gestures, also known as the vocabulary. The vocabulary in this case is relatively easy to create since it only involves 2D static gestures. The complexity of the solution increases as dynamic gestures are involved and tracking is required for both detecting movement as well as depth. The Kinect, for example, uses two cameras and an IR sensor (in its implementation) to identify hand and body poses in 3D environments.

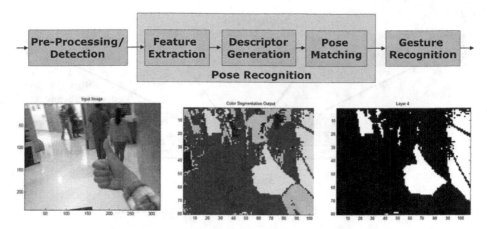

*Figure 2-22.* *Hand pose detection and recognition flow*

## 2.4.3 Video Summarization

Video summarization refers to the ability to analyze a full video and summarizing it by either (a) extracting the salient segments of the video with a small number of frames or video snippets or (b) creating a short transcript of the video by identifying the series of activities in the video. The usage could range from video surveillance, where the anomalies are the salient scenes in the video, OR event summaries such as identifying the key parts of soccer game (like the goals or the major attempts). In this section, we will focus on the former and describe the approaches used to identifying salient portions of a video and to potentially classify the activity.

There are multiple approaches in the literature on how to identify salient frames. A simple way to think of it is to figure out which frames in the video best represent the scenarios in the video while at the same time identifying just enough number of frames unique from each other. Many approaches rely on color, motion, or other low-level feature detectors. Some also focus on boundary detection, where a significant change between frames indicates a potential salient event. Using these techniques, one can identify salient frames in the video, but these may represent too many frames or too few frames depending on how different or similar the frames are to each other.

Recent efforts have been focusing on using a combination of diversity and coverage metrics to determine how to end with a finite number of frames in the video that represents both sufficient coverage as well as sufficient diversity amongst each other. One approach by S. Chakraborty et al. tries to do better by adaptively determining the summary length as well as the frames to pick within that summary. In this paper, the authors propose an adaptive summarization technique that poses this problem as an optimization problem for selecting a set of sufficiently unique frames representing the video. The optimization problem considers representativeness and uniqueness as the two key metrics and tries to maximize both metrics to identify keyframes in an adaptive manner. Figure 2-23 illustrates the basic idea. They compare it to a traditional mechanisms, such as random sampling, clustering, and the use of curvature points, and show that it is more effective.

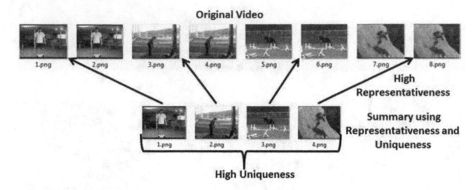

*Figure 2-23.* *Example video summarization (from S. Chakraborty et al.)*

Recent efforts attempt to consider semantic context of the video by employing convolutional neural networks (CNNs) to identify entities (multiple objects, locations, people, and activities) and scoring these entities with respect to their co-occurrence as well as relation to the type of classification scenario of importance. They show that this approach has significant potential since it is semantically more meaningful and effective. An example flow of this video summarization technique is shown in Figure 2-24.

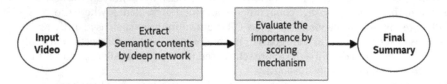

*Figure 2-24.* *Example video summarization using deep networks*

Overall, video summarization based on visual information is quite a challenging and important problem and the existing literature is just getting started in providing a suitable set of summarization schemes. We refer the reader to the papers in the reference section of this chapter to get a better understanding of techniques in this area along with applied usage scenarios.

# 2.5   Other Sensors

There are a large number of sensors beyond the ones covered in more detail above. Below is a summary of these sensors and their potential usages.

## 2.5.1   Proximity Sensor

A proximity sensor detects the presence of an object in the vicinity without having to touch the object. Typically, a proximity sensor is IR (infrared)-based and it works by sensing the change in the IR field. An example of proximity sensor usage is in phones to determine whether the phone is up against your ear due to a call in order to avoid any accidental touches during that time. Another example is the use of a proximity sensor in robots to determine whether it is coming close to an obstacle and therefore needs to move around it or turn around. In addition to IR proximity sensors, wireless solutions such as BLE and Wi-Fi devices may also be used to determine whether a device is within the proximity of a beacon or an access point. Since this is also location related, it covered in more detail in the next section.

## 2.5.2   Location Sensor

A location sensor helps determine the geographical location of a device. The most common location sensor is the GPS (global positioning system) sensor that is used very frequently in navigation systems within cars as well as phones. The GPS system communicates with the satellites orbiting around the earth and uses trilateration to determine the location of the device that consists of the GPS receiver. This is very useful for outdoor location, but does not work well for indoor location. For indoor location, similar radio-based approaches can be used but with Wi-Fi access points as the triangulation point or BLE beacons that are becoming increasingly popular.

## 2.5.3   Touch sensors

Touch sensors are common these days in all wearable watches, phones and tablets, and are even available on laptop screens these days. Touch screens serve the purpose of allowing users to interact with screens with their finger rather than the mouse. The use of fingers makes the experience much easier and intuitive. Touch screens can be resistive or capacitive—the former (resistive) uses resistance between multiple layers and your finger as the way of identifying the touch, whereas the latter (capacitive) uses the flow of electricity between your fingers and the screen as the way of determining touch. Recent efforts are further improving touch screen resolution by incorporating force (how far do you press the finger) as another key input into the experience.

## 2.5.4   Magnetic Sensors

Magnetic field sensors or magnetometers detect and measure the magnetic field with different levels of sensitivity depending on the type of sensor used. A common magnetometer is the Hall Effect sensor that changes its output voltage depending on the intensity of the magnetic field. The Hall sensor can be used in industrial applications to sense the presence of magnetic objects as well as measure the timing of their arrival/departure.

## 2.5.5   Chemical and Biosensors

A growing field of sensing is the use of chemical and biosensors. Chemical sensors are used for sensing the composition of gas or liquids. These are immensely useful for analyzing air quality and gas presence in industrial environments. Biosensing targets the presence of cells, protein, nucleic acid, etc. This can be used to analyze skin conditions, for example. Use of both chemical and biosensing is becoming extremely attractive for usages in environmental, industrial, health, and wellness applications.

## 2.6 Summary

In this chapter, we reviewed three types of sensors (IMU, audio and visual) and walked through the processing phases to process the raw sensor data and convert it into recognized information. Through the process, we discussed the key components involved in the processing and the many algorithms used to trade-off accuracy and computing complexity. For example, we showed that visual processing and recognition ranges from object recognition from a simple 2D image to video summarization across many frames. In the coming chapter, we will discuss how these sensors can be used together for multi-modal processing as well as how to convert recognized information into actionable knowledge.

## 2.7 References

- Mak, Man-Wai and Hon-Bill Yu. "A study of voice activity detection techniques for NIST speaker recognition evaluations." *Journal Computer Speech and Language* 28 no. 1 (2014).

- Lee, S. , Zhang, Y. et al. "Accelerating Mobile Augmented Reality on a Handheld Platform." ICCD 2009.

- Bay, H., Tuytelaars, T. and L. Van Gool. "Surf: Speeded Up Robust Features." *ECCV06*, (2006): 427–434.

- Lowe, D. G. "Distinctive Image Features from Scale-Invariant Keypoints."*Int. J. Comput. Vision*, 60, no. 2 (2004): 91–110.

- Rublee, E., Rabaud, V., Konolige, K. and G. R. Bradski. "ORB: an efficient alternative to SIFT or SURF." *ICCV* (2011).

- Rosten, E. and T. Drummond. "Machine learning for high-speed corner detection." *ECCV* (2006).

- Calonder, M., Lepetit, V., Strecha, C. and P. Fua. "BRIEF: Binary Robust Independent Elementary Features." *ECCV* (2010).

- Leutenegger, S., Chli, M. and R. Siegwart. "Brisk: Binary Robust Invariant Scalable Keypoints." *ICCV* (2011).

- Chakraborty, S., Tickoo, O., and Ravi Iyer. "Adaptive Keyframe Selection for Video Summarization." IEEE Winter Conference on Applications of Computer Vision (WACV 2015), Oct. 2015.

- Prahlad, K. "Speech Technology: A Practical Introduction." http://www.speech.cs.cmu.edu/15-492/slides/03_mfcc.pdf

- Breebaart, J. and M. McKinney. "Features for audio classification. Proc. SOIA2002, Philips Symposium on Intelligent Algorithms." Eindhoven, 2002.

- Hwangbo, M., Alan, T., Tickoo, O. and R. Iyer. "Low-complexity HOG for efficient video saliency." International Conference on Image Processing (ICIP 2015).

# CHAPTER 3

■ ■ ■

# Multimodal Recognition

In the last chapter, we introduced processing of each type of raw sensor data independently to realize different levels of recognition capabilities. We found that inertial sensors provide information about movement across different axes. Audio streams can be processed not only for sound types but also words and natural language. We also showed how to recognize different objects, faces, activities, and more. Now we imagine what is possible if we were able to correlate the understanding across multiple sensor types simultaneously. This is referred to as "multi-modal recognition" and we will walk through different methods for multi-modal recognition in this chapter.

## 3.1 Why Multi-modality

Figure 3-1 introduces the benefits of multi-modal recognition using the same three sensor types (inertial, audio, and visual) as an example.

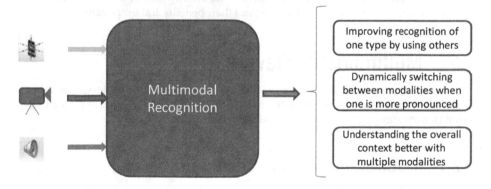

*Figure 3-1.* *Introduction to multi-modal recognition*

The benefits of multi-modal recognition starts with the ability to improve the recognition in one type of modality (e.g., sound) and by using other modalities to assist (visual). This is particularly effective when the recognition capability is either impaired, needs clarification, or needs efficiency. For example, when you hear "turn that off," in order to understand what "that" implies, it is important to use the visual recognition to

© Omesh Tickoo and Ravi Iyer 2017
O. Tickoo and R. Iyer, *Making Sense of Sensors*, DOI 10.1007/978-1-4302-6593-1_3

determine what the user is pointing towards. In this case, the visual recognition provided clarification for disambiguating the indirection "that" to a particular thing like a fan or a light. In addition to this, it is also possible to use one modality to improve the processing efficiency of the other. Let's consider a retail example where the user needs help with a particular type of product. If he or she is already in the aisle and just needs to check the price of an item, it is easy to reduce the speech processing efficiency if we are able to reduce the lookup vocabulary to only commands that pertain to that type of usage. This is possible by using visual cues regarding the location of the user by determining the type of products he or she is glancing at. This type of example will be used later in this chapter to understand the type of multi-modal recognition needed to be able to accomplish this.

Another benefit of multi-modal recognition is to use multiple modalities dynamically depending on which one is more effective. For example, when processing a (soccer game) video for summarization, there are parts that are visually appealing (a powerful kick by a favorite player) and parts that are rich in sound (e.g., commentator announcing a goal along with applause from the audience). Both modalities can be used to better understand each video segment of interest. By considering the audio and video recognition modalities independently first and correlating events of interest, this can be achieved quite easily. Alternatively, the recognition can be done at a finer granularity if there is interest in correlating the player (visually recognized) with their name (speech recognition based on commentator audio).

It should be noted that, as humans, we handle these modalities quite naturally and cross-correlate between them to determine context. We tend to achieve this at different levels of granularity depending on the usage and context. For example, we can handle sounds, movement, and visual input while driving a bike through a park, for instance. The challenge is to achieve the same level of recognition and efficiency with computing machines by dynamically switching between different granularities of recognition and different levels of coupling between the different modalities as required. This is a hard problem, but as described below, can be solved if we classify each of the types of multi-modal recognition individually and understand their benefits and usage contexts.

# 3.2 Multimodality Flavors

In this section we present different approaches and frameworks used to design the sensor fusion solutions. We mainly cover the following three widely used approaches: coupling-based classification, Dasarathy model, and sensor configuration model.

## 3.2.1 Coupling-based Classification

Information from multiple sensor sources can be combined at various stages in the recognition chain. For the sake of simplicity, let us consider two sensors processing pipelines as shown in Figure 3-2. In Figure 3-2, both the processing pipes operate independently of each other. The exact locations on each pipeline where the sensor fusion can occur depend on various factors including the implementation complexity and the desired accuracy for the recognition task. We define three main levels of sensor data fusion.

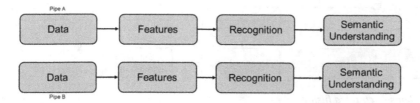

**Figure 3-2.** *Two sensor processing pipelines*

- Uncoupled sensor data fusion/Semantic Fusion: The definition refers to the case where the data fusion occurs at the last possible stage in the respective pipelines. This usually means integration after the recognition is done, as shown in Figure 3-3. The advantage of this method is that the sensor fusion is simple and can be accomplished using existing technology pipelines for recognition. Domain experts like this approach because cross-domain technical knowledge requirements are minimal. It is generally very hard to find technology experts that can master more than one sensor domain. For semantic fusion approaches, the domain experts can work independently and the application developers can integrate the modalities at the higher level.

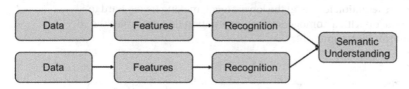

**Figure 3-3.** *Uncoupled fusion*

- Loosely coupled sensor data fusion/Restricted recognition: To get performance advantage over uncoupled sensor fusion, experts rely on a mode that restricts the recognition search space of mode modality based on the results from the other. In this approach, one recognition pipe helps to set the context for the other. Once that is accomplished, the second recognition pipe need only perform recognition within the established context boundaries, leading to potential savings in compute and higher performance. Figure 3-4 illustrates this. The inter-domain expertise requirement is minimal, as in the case of semantic sensor fusion, but the developer does need to understand the semantic dependence of recognition between modes.

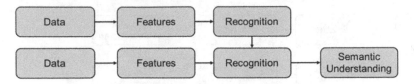

*Figure 3-4.* *Loosely coupled fusion*

- Tightly coupled sensor data fusion/data-feature level fusion: This most performance-friendly model of sensor fusion allows for virtual combination of multiple sensors in such a manner that the combined sensors appear as a single complex sensor for most of the application stack. As shown in Figure 3-5, the methods of sensor integration include combining the raw data from sensors and using a single data stream for processing. More practical methods combine features from the sensors to produce a single feature set for recognition and filtering. While the tight integration provides the most performance boost for sensor fusion usages, this method is not very popular due to the requirement for multi-domain experts to work on data integration. Data representation at the lower levels of stack is very sensor-specific, so experts are needed to make sensible decisions for merging data from multiple sources. Each sensor model has a different data representation format at the lowest level, making it very hard to come up with a homogenous representation that preserves the information content.

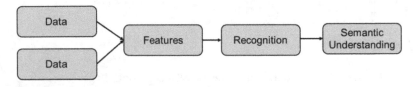

*Figure 3-5.* *Tightly coupled fusion*

## 3.2.2 Dasarathy Model

An elegant model to represent different levels of data fusion was proposed by Dasarathy (see references at the end of the chapter for the original proposal information). It represents different approaches to data fusion as a function of input and output data types, resulting in the following different types of fusion.

- Data In-Data Out (DAI-DAO): The DAI-DAO model represents the low-level fusion, where the sensor data from multiple sensors is fused together to produce a fused data representation for the rest of the recognition pipeline. The format of the resulting data can be the same as the input (in the case of fusing similar sensors), or an entirely new format (heterogeneous sensor fusion).

- Data In-Feature Out (DAI-FEO): In this model, the fusion engine takes as input the data from sources to be fused and produces as output a feature set that represents the combined information from the sensors. This hybrid approach sits between the low- and mid-level fusion approaches.

- Feature In-Feature Out (FEI-FEO): In the FEI-FEO model, the fusion engine combines pre-extracted features from different sensors. The output is a feature set combining the multiple feature inputs. This method represents mid-level sensor fusion.

- Feature In-Decision Out (FEI-DEO): In this context, "decision" refers to recognition of the sensor data. This method is a hybrid between the mid-level and high-level data fusion techniques. The fusion engine in this case takes features from different sensor pipelines as an input and combines these to provide the recognition (decision) output.

- Decision In-Decision Out (DEI-DEO): This model is the high-level sensor fusion model also referred to as semantic fusion by us in the discussion above. Typically, this kind of sensor fusion is the easiest type of fusion since we are not actually "fusing" anything. The fusion engine in most cases will "combine" the recognized information from the pipelines to come to a recognition decision.

## 3.2.3    Sensor Configuration Model

Based on the sensor configuration model, multimodal sensor fusion can improve the functional accuracy of recognition through one of the following modes. Figure 3-6 illustrates the interaction between different sensor pipes for these modes.

- Complimentary Fusion: In complementary sensor fusion, two or more sensors are used to recognize information that is not possible to be extracted from individual sensors alone. The sensor fusion has an additive effect in this case.

- Redundant Fusion: In this mode, sensor fusion uses two or more sensors to provide information about the same underlying process to introduce redundancy in the recognition.

- Cooperative Fusion: In cooperative sensor fusion, different information about the same underlying process is gathered using different sensors before being combined to get better recognition of the underlying process, as opposed to single sensor-based solutions.

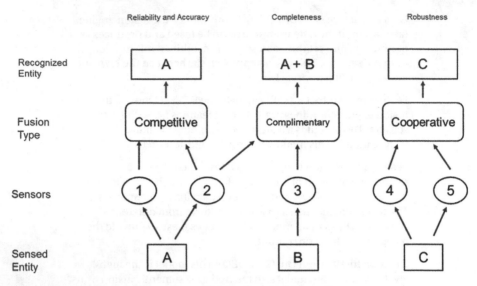

***Figure 3-6.*** *Fusion based on sensor collaboration model*

# 3.3  Example Implementations

In this section we present examples of the different flavors of multimodal sensor integration as described in the section above. We will use the audio and visual sensors as examples, but the approaches are extensible to other types of heterogeneous sensors as well.

## 3.3.1  Semantic Fusion

Consider a usage involving human-machine interaction with a user trying to employ gestures and speech for interacting with a computer or a robot. For example, a user might be pointing to an object in the camera field of view and asking about the properties of the object using voice.

This scenario involves merging the recognition results from the visual and audio streams to realize the usage. Figure 3-7 shows the data flow.

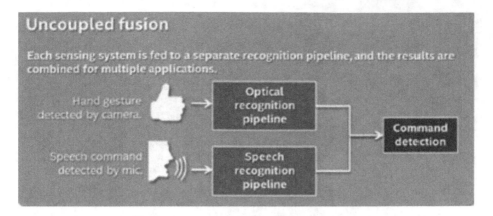

**Figure 3-7.** *Semantic fusion for hand gesture-based voice commands*

As shown in Figure 3-7, two recognition pipes are independent and complete, as described separately in Chapter 2. The fusion occurs at the semantic level, i.e., at a level after the basic recognition is over, and we are dealing with semantics/meaning of the data.

## 3.3.2   Restricted Recognition

Restricted recognition improves recognition performance for multiple modes by "restricting" the domain of search for one of the recognition modes. Consider a connected audio-visual query system that can provide details in real time about the objects that a user points her camera at. The usage involves pointing a smart camera at an unknown object and asking a verbal query about the object. Queries like "What is that object?", "What is the cheapest price of that book?", "How are the reviews of this book?", etc., can be supported. After the query is "understood" using the speech recognition technology and the target object of the query is identified, the system performs an online search to retrieve the response. Another step may be involved to format the result and present it to the user in a predefined manner.

Such a usage can benefit from restricted recognition through performance and response time improvements. The high level concept is shown in Figure 3-8. Basically, having the context from one mode can improve the performance of the second mode considerably. For example, if the speech recognition engine has difficulty in confidently recognizing the uttered speech, using the context from recognized visual objects can improve speech recognition. If the speech recognition engine returns the query string as "How are the reviews for this hook?" and the recognition confidence score is below a predetermined threshold, the fact that a visual recognition module reports a "book" in the current recognized objects can be used to correct the query to "How are the reviews for this book?"

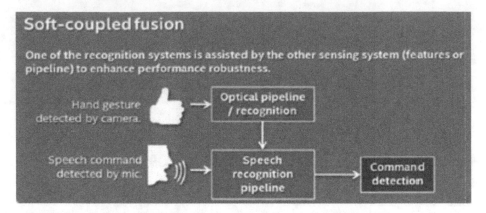

*Figure 3-8.* *Restricted recognition for hand gesture-based voice commands*

### 3.3.3    Tight Fusion

Multiple sensors use a unified recognition flow in this case. The data from different modes is combined very early in the process. Raw data, filtered data, or features may be fused. A single recognition classifier acts on the fused data for recognition. As an example, let us revisit the audio-visual sensor fusion example from above. Instead of improving the speech recognition performance after the visual recognition is done, if we modify the pipeline as shown in Figure 3-9, the recognition module will take the combined inputs from the audio and visual modes and provide recognition based on the combined data.

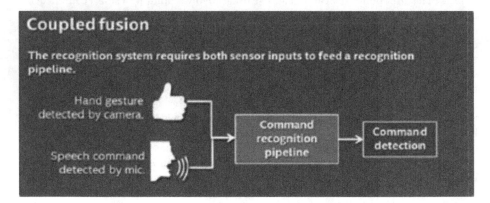

*Figure 3-9.* *Tight coupled fusion for hand gesture-based voice commands*

This form of recognition has the potential to provide the most performance improvement by eliminating duplication of recognition between modes. However, this is also the hardest to implement method due to multiple reasons, including:

- Lack of cross-domain experts: In the example above we would need experts from speech recognition and visual computing technologies to work closely together. It is relatively rare to find individual experts having deep technical knowledge of both domains.

- Different data formats: Different modes use different types of data and feature representations, making it a challenge to effectively combine these without loss of relevant information.

- Lack of training data: To effectively train the models for multi-modal recognition, we need multi-modal training data. Such data is hard to get from traditional data sources and one needs to generate data by artificially constructing scenarios. This type of training data generation poses significant scalability challenges.

# 3.4　Mathematical Approaches for Sensor Fusion

Sensor fusion enables better recognition through multiple approaches. The two main approaches are through inference and estimation. Inference assumes that the nature of the process generating the input signals is known in advance, so the obtained data can be used to infer the entity being recognized. Inferencing can also be interpreted as a form of decision fusion, since a decision is taken based on the knowledge of the perceived situation. Estimation, on the other hand, deals with trying to deduce (or recognize) the nature of the process producing the data given the observed nature of the data. In the following pages we will present a very brief overview of some of the common methods used for inference and estimation. The discussion here is neither exhaustive nor descriptive enough, and interested readers are encouraged to follow the references for deeper understanding of the topics.

## 3.4.1　Inferencing Approaches

- Bayesian Inference. Bayesian inference uses the famous Bayes rule to recognize the target entity based on observed data. The Bayes rule describes the probability of an event based on the prior knowledge of conditions that may be related to the event in varying degrees. For multi-modal sensor fusion, this method uses the prior knowledge about co-occurrences of input values to determine occurrence of the event being recognized. The method is very popular in situations where accurate recognition is needed under relatively controlled conditions. The availability of controlled conditions makes it possible to obtain a lot of training data, making it possible to make accurate decisions.

- Dampster-Shaefer Inference. The Dampseter-Shaefer inference method is based on the Theory of Evidence and does away with the need for a priori probabilities of unknown propositions. This makes it possible to use the method for inference in conditions where all the possible combinations of the input signals along with their relationship to the fused output are not known in advance. The Dampseter-Shaefer inference method provides flexibility of implementation in various conditions. This method, however, sacrifices accuracy for flexibility when compared to the Bayesian methods.

- Fuzzy Logic-based Inference: In many instances of sensor fusion one may have to deal with data that does not fit well into traditional quantification models. For example, given two sensors, Sensor A and Sensor B, one may want to define inference models based on conditions like "Sensor A reports a HIGH value and Sensor B is NOISY." In such cases, Fuzzy Logic-based sensor fusion systems try to find the best outcome using the varying or dependent parameters as input variables.

The Fuzzy Logic systems work in three different steps as shown in Figure 3-10. The steps are:

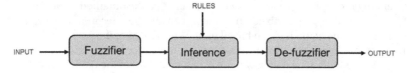

***Figure 3-10.*** *Fuzzy Logic-based inference*

1. Fuzzification: The fuzzification process involves assigning the input various pre-defined input classes. For each input, the step determines a "degree of membership" to each class based on defined boundaries. The degree of membership is a value between 0 and 1 and defines the state of input at any time.

2. Inference: The rule-based inference step uses the input state to arrive at an inferred result. For example, the applied inference rule could state that "if Sensor A is HIGH and Sensor B is NOISY then use Sensor A output to update the results from Sensor B."

3. Defuzzification: This last step in the process takes the inferred output and applied inference rules to generate a measurable output of the sensor fusion system. For the example above, the defuzzification step could apply predefined mathematical models to update Sensor B data based on Sensor A output.

Neural Network-based inference: In various places you will find neural networks described as "computing systems made up of simple, highly connected processing elements which process information by their dynamic state response to external inputs." The neural networks (NNs) or Artificial Neural Networks (ANNs), as they are referred to frequently, are modeled after the neuronal structure of the human cerebral cortex. However, the scale of ANNs is much smaller compared to a human brain (thousands of neurons for a large ANN vs. billions of neurons in a human brain). Architecturally, the ANNs are composed of layers of neurons. The "input layer" consists of neurons that accept the data from various sensors. The data then is processed by one or more "hidden layers" before being presented to the user through the "output layer." Each layer consists of a number of interconnected nodes with activation functions for processing. The connections between the nodes are weighted functions (Figure 3-11). The ANNs have to go through a "training" or "learning" phase before they can be used for inferencing (or classification). The learning rule modifies the weights of the connections according to the input patterns presented. The learning is achieved through examples where the correct desired outputs are known in advance. The ANNs are presented with an input set from all the sensors. ANN will try to "guess" the correct output. The training procedure then calculates the error between the ANN output and the ideal desired output and uses this error to update the ANN connection weights. A new input is then presented and the procedure repeated until the weights converge to values for satisfactory results. Of course, the actual procedure is far more involved, but this high-level procedural overview will suffice for our discussion on sensor fusion methods. ANN-based inferencing approaches have the advantage that example-based learning does not depend on knowing the actual relationships between the inputs and outputs. Hence, the approach is very useful in conditions where we seek robustness in the face of noise; discover relationships between sets of patterns; input volume, number, or diversity is great; or input relationships are vague and poorly described with conventional approaches.

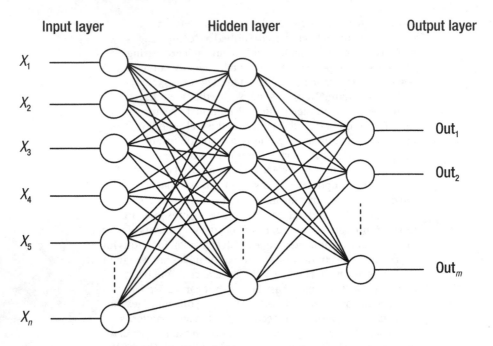

**Figure 3-11.** *Artificial Neural Network*

## 3.4.2    Estimation Approaches

Given a set of observations, the estimation techniques tend to derive the parameters of the underlying process producing the observations. In the case of multi-modal sensor fusion applications, the observations consist of combined information from multiple sensor processes. The popular estimation methods assume that the underlying process is an unknown linear process. The observations are a combination of the process outputs in time along with white noise. Least squares estimation is the most popular estimation method and is described below.

- Least Squares: Given a number of observations, least squares method aims to find the "best fit" line representing these observations. The line is taken to be the representation of the underlying process (and additive noise). This method is the most flexible of a family of such methods in that it assumes no prior information about the process probability density of the noise. This method gets its name from the fact that the estimation aims to minimize the least squares error between the measurements and the estimated process.

## 3.5 Summary

In this chapter we introduced the concept of multi-modality and how it can be used to improve recognition performance over single mode recognition. We discussed different uses of multi-modality and how it can spur new recognition-based usages in addition to improving the existing ones. We briefly touched upon a few techniques to achieve multi-modal recognition under various conditions and architecture goals. The reader is encouraged to follow the references in the next section for more in-depth information about these techniques. The next chapter will focus on yet another way to improve recognition performance, i.e., through the use of context.

## 3.6 References

- Nakamura, Eduardo F. and Antonio A. F. Loureiro. "Information Fusion for Wireless Sensor Networks: Methods, Models, and Classifications" *ACM Computing Surveys*. 39, no. 3 (2007).

- Koneru, Ujwal; Redkar, Sangram, and Anshuman Razdan. "Fuzzy Logic Based Sensor Fusion for Accurate Tracking." In *Proceedings of the 7th International Conference on Advances in Visual Computing - Volume Part II.*

- Shafer, G. *A Mathematical Theory of Evidence*. Princeton, NJ: Princeton University Press, 1976.

- Bass, T. "Intrusion Detection Systems and Multisensor Data Fusion: Creating Cyberspace Situational Awareness." *Communications of the ACM* 43, no. 4 (2000): 99–105.

- Bayes, T. "An Essay towards Solving a Problem in the Doctrine of Chances." *Philosophical Transactions of the Royal Society of London* 53 (1763): 370–418. Reprinted in *Biometrika*, 45, (1958): 293–315.

- Bedworth, M. D. and J. O'Brien. "The Omnibus Model: A New Architecture for Data Fusion?" Proceedings of the 2nd International Conference on Information Fusion (FUSION'99), Helsinki, Finland, July 1999.

- Blackman, S. S. "Multiple Sensor Tracking and Data Fusion." In *Introduction to Sensor Systems*. Norwood, MA: Artech House, 1988.

- Brooks, R. R. and S. S. Iyengar. *Multi-Sensor Fusion: Fundamentals and Applications*. NJ: Prentice Hall, 1998.

- Buede, D. M. "Shafer-Dempster and Bayesian reasoning: a response to 'Shafer-Dempster reasoning with applications to multisensor target identification systems.'" *IEEE Transactions on Systems, Man, and Cybernetics* 18, no. 6 (1988): 1009–1011.

- Dasarathy, B. V. "Information fusion - what, where, why, when, and how?" *Information Fusion* 2, no. 2 (2001): 75–76.

# CHAPTER 4

■■■

# Contextual Recognition

In this chapter we move beyond the primary theme of recognition and begin to understand what the next level of understanding looks like. Specifically, we will discuss the concept of "context" and contextual understanding. In simple terms, context refers to the environment under which we are trying to understand something. Having contextual information allows for better recognition, as we discussed in the case of multi-modal sensor fusion in Chapter 3. Conversely, having a recognition of specific environmental attributes can help us define context that can aid in understanding of the scene being observed. Some examples of contextual recognition are outlined below:

- Having an understanding of the environment allows for recognition of objects that are occluded and hard for traditional algorithms to recognize. For example, recognizing a table and a monitor makes it easy to recognize a keyboard on the table even if the keyboard is occluded and not easy to be recognized in isolation.

- A recognition system can benefit from knowing the relationships between different objects. For example, in many pictures an office chair always faces a table. This semantic positional relationship between the chair and the table can allow for optimized recognition of one object after we have recognized the other.

- Contextual recognition can help predict occluded objects in a scene. For example, detecting a feline tail occluded behind a tree can be predicted as a tiger cub or a large cat depending on the context based on location (forest vs. park)

## 4.1 Relationship between Context and Recognition

In this section we try to bridge the gap between recognition and context in the "forward" direction, i.e., we will understand how one can deduce context from recognition.

There are two main types of systems that deal with contextual recognition, namely rule-based systems and knowledge-based systems. Contextual information forms the basis of the difference between rule-based and knowledge-based systems. Before we understand the importance of context, we present a very high-level overview of these two

© Omesh Tickoo and Ravi Iyer 2017
O. Tickoo and R. Iyer, *Making Sense of Sensors*, DOI 10.1007/978-1-4302-6593-1_4

types of systems. The actual in-depth discussion is deferred to the later chapters. Also, we will only concentrate on the object recognition from images as the goal and leave the more complicated usage goals for later chapters.

Goal: Given a picture, identify the objects in the image.

### 4.1.1   Rule-based Systems

Rule-based systems work as explained in the previous chapters, where the systems works in an "if XX then YY" manner. The image is broken down into features, and the features are analyzed by algorithms looking for a pretrained pattern between them. If the pattern matches a training example or generally falls "close" to some trained rule of representation, the recognition is deemed to be a success, otherwise the target object is declared to be not present in the scene.

### 4.1.2   Knowledge-based Systems

In case of knowledge-based systems, the system uses prior information to determine the recognition result. The probability of something being recognized increases as the system finds more and more related information in a given input. Such systems use the prior observed correlations between observations to determine the possibility of a recognition match. Many times such knowledge-based systems will use the correlation information to determine if and what parts of a given input are worth searching for, a recognition match using the rule-based methods. Such hybrid approaches have been shown to be highly effective in optimizing the performance of recognition systems both in terms of speed of execution as well as accuracy.

## 4.2   Understanding Context

Context is composed of the aggregate of information within which the recognition occurs. For example, if an algorithm is looking to identify an instance of a keyboard in an image, the context could comprise of the scene in the image (forest, city, office, etc.). In case of a picture of the forest, the context gives a clue that finding the keyboard is unlikely. Alternately, if the context of the scene in the image points to it being a computer desk, the chances are that the keyboard can be found with higher probability. Further contextual clues can then be employed to localize the region of search (below the monitor, on the table, etc.).

Context also helps humans to perform recognition or react to different scenarios. As an example, observing an animal part (a tail) with the actual animal hiding from the view behind a tree can elicit responses from a human observer that vary based on the context. A person observing the occluded animal above in a park will most likely behave differently than a person observing the same in a forest. The scene around the observation in this case provides the context for recognition (harmless pet vs. a wild animal).

## 4.2.1    Different Roles for Context

Context as a concept can take multiple roles in recognition. Briefly, any form that provides information about the environment of a target entity can contribute to context. Some examples are given below:

- Semantic Context: Several entities can be contextually related by virtue of them being part of the same environment. Similarly, if the entities are not generally part of the same environment, they do not share a semantic context among themselves. It is highly likely to find a computer keyboard in an image that contains a computer monitor as well vs. an image of a sunny beach. In this example, monitor and keyboard are semantically related while the beach and keyboard are semantically unrelated.

- Spatial Context: Spatial context refers to the spatial arrangement of objects or items of interest to recognition with respect to each other. As an example, spatially a tree or a fire hydrant will always be above the ground. A keyboard will mostly be placed under the monitor and a sidewalk will be situated on the side of a street. Spatial context makes it possible to reduce the search space for target object recognition if we happen to identify other spatially related objects in a scene.

- Pose-based Context: Many objects are not just related in spatial context but also depict pose-based consistency toward each other. A dining chair usually faces the table, cars on the same side of the road usually face in the same direction as each other, etc. Adding the pose-based context information to spatial context can further reduce the recognition system complexity by introducing semantic clues for inter-object recognition.

# 4.3    Including Context in Recognition

The benefits of using context for recognition purposes can be explained by the following metrics:

- Accuracy: Having contextual information from a scene can assist in more accurate recognition. Knowing that the scene depicts a beach can help recognize an object as a beach ball vs. some kind of a fruit (melon).

The three remaining benefits are a direct result of the reduction of search space both spatially as well as in the target set of entities considered based on context.

- Power: The amount of power spent by a compute device to recognize an object can be reduced drastically by using the scene context to restrict the search space for target objects. The objects that do not contextually belong to the scene can be eliminated from the target search space.

- Speed: Having a smaller search space also leads to faster recognition times.

- Compute: The compute resources needed to recognize scale down with the search space as well.

A modified form of a recognition pipeline from Chapter 1 with contextual block is presented in Figure 4-1 below.

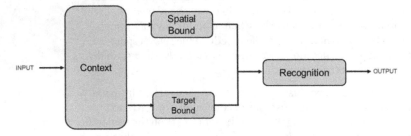

**Figure 4-1.** *Incorporating context in recognition*

The flow shows a few new processing modules between the scene data and the recognition. Context block uses predefined and trained methods to determine the context of the scene. Based on the scene context, the spatial bounding module restricts the search space in the input to the regions that are most probable to contain the target entities (using pose, spatial, and semantic contexts as described earlier). The target bound processing reduces the sample space to match the image features based on the context information. The result of this contextual bound processing is a highly optimized and fast recognition block.

# 4.4 Motivation from Human Recognition

The concept of contextual recognition borrows heavily from human recognition. Various studies have shown that humans are very fast in recognizing different entities and situations because of a very fast and optimized contextual search capability. As described for the computer-based recognition above, humans depict recognition based on both environmental scene context and spatial context.

## 4.4.1   Image-based Contextual Recognition

In a recent study, the human subjects were asked to describe the scene in a blurred street image. A majority of the people responded with observing a street scene with a car and a pedestrian <Reference>. In reality, the image was created with the same car image in two positions tilted 90 degrees. The common majority response of the test observers recognizing the car as a pedestrian is an effect of human contextual observation where a person expects a pedestrian in such a scene. The above example also shows that in some cases context can be a distraction making the problem hard to solve. Thankfully such cases are much smaller in number compared to the scenes where context is helpful in recognition. In the example above contextual recognition fails in a scene that is synthetic and very improbable at best.

Similarly, asking a group of observers to perform a people search in a presented image and tracking their attention through gaze trackers produced an average heat map that can be seen as a modulated saliency map. The saliency map shows that the human attention quickly focuses on a few areas in the picture to look for objects of interest. Contextually, that is the location in the picture where the chances of finding the target objects are the highest, making it the right place to focus the search. The search methodology for humans is not uniform across the image but, once the parts of the scene are identified coarsely, the search quickly focuses on the areas most likely to contain the target entity. Comparing with machines, when looking for an object in a scene, studies have shown that the observers casually scan the scene and fixate the search on regions that contextually have the highest probability of containing the object in question. The majority of the objects are recognized in a glance before eye fixation.

Consistency-inconsistency effect: Accuracy of object detection (as measured by speed of detection) is improved if the object is presented after a contextual scene, for example, bread followed by kitchen or wild animals in a forest.

## 4.4.2   Non-image-based Contextual Recognition

As an example of a non-visual recognition task, consider the following sentence:

"Aoccdrnig to a rscheearch at Cmabrigde Uinervtisy, it deosn't mttaer in waht oredr the ltteers in a wrod are, the olny iprmoetnt tihng is taht the frist and lsat ltteer be at the rghit pclae. The rset can be a toatl mses and you can sitll raed it wouthit porbelm. Tihs is bcuseae the huamn mnid deos not raed ervey lteter by istlef, but the wrod as a wlohe."

Clearly, the words in the sentence above are misspelled, but the readers do not find it difficult to read the intent of the sentence. In many cases the readers are able to "read" the later words faster than the earlier ones. This is due to the contextual nature of the human understanding, where we expect the words to fit the context and the expectation from the next word in the sentence. The noise in the input above is effectively countered by the contextual human inference.

The sentences are understood even if some words are misspelled. In fact, if the number of alphabets and the first and last alphabets are preserved, all the words can be misspelled.

# 4.5 Contextual Recognition: From Humans to Machines

Extending the analogy to computer systems, a contextual recognition system exploits the fact that objects never occur in isolation and are usually part of particular environments. It is generally easier do a quick evaluation of input data that use different sensors to get an understanding of the operating environment than to identify occurrence of some target objects with varying granularities in the image. Statistical summary of the scene provides a complimentary and an effective source of information for contextual inference. In particular, knowing the context helps to improve recognition in presence of the following data imperfections as well (Figure 4-2, 4-3):

- Noisy Data: The input data can be contaminated by noise due to imperfect sensor or non-conducive environmental conditions. Noisy data can make the feature generation process very difficult. Traditionally, various filtering methods are used to smoothen the noisy data before processing. While the filter-based smoothening methods usually achieve good results for human observations (e.g., visually pleasing images), they usually present significant challenges for automated computer-based recognition. Having context information handy makes it easier for the computer recognition methods to ignore the noise and look for features that may actually depict the real world information.

- Occluded Data: As described earlier, non-contextual recognition methods fail to process information that is occluded by other information from the sensors. However, having the contextual information makes it possible to make speculative recognition work based on incomplete recognition information from occluded data.

- Poor Resolution: Sometimes the sensors are not able to capture a target image with enough high fidelity for the recognition algorithms to work properly. The reasons for this vary from the object being too far from the sensor range to poor sensor parameters. Having the context information helps to compensate for the poor data resolution by augmenting incomplete information with the probabilistic model of the target object being present.

- Cluttered scenes: In cluttered scenes, the segmentation of objects becomes a problem for recognition algorithms. However, having the context for the scene can reduce the problem to a smaller target region that can be analyzed more efficiently.

- Object pose variability: The recognition algorithms are only as good as the diversity of the data they have been trained with. It is practically impossible to train an algorithm will all types of possible poses, angles, and environments that the target object might present itself in. Having contextual recognition capability helps recognize object configurations that may vary to some degree from the trained models.

- Illumination changes: Similar to the pose changes, the training data cannot account for different illumination conditions under which an object maybe observed. For non-visual tasks, this amounts to observing target phenomenon under varying environments. Having context information can help reduce the effects of such environmental variations.

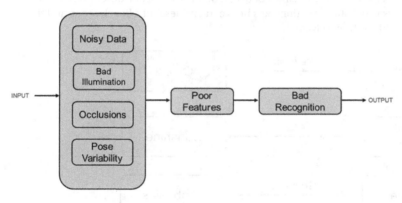

*Figure 4-2.* *Bad sensor data can cause problems in recognition*

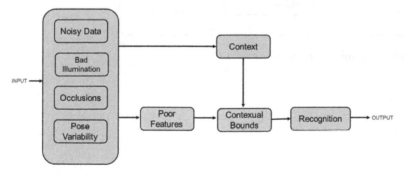

*Figure 4-3.* *Context can help reduce effects of bad sensor data*

63

# 4.6    Representing Context

By now we understand the need and importance of context in recognition. This section addresses the problems in effectively using context for recognition in real and practical systems. Two such main issues are:

1.    simple representations for context

2.    algorithms that can extract and use such context

While the detailed discussion of the methods is left for later chapters, we briefly touch upon how the representation for context can be carried out. In short, the context representation is distilled down to the problem of relationships between different objects and scenes. Analogous to the triplet-based relationship reorientation discussed in the first chapter, the context can be represented in the form of relationships between different entities in the scene or the relationships between objects and scene description itself. Figure 4-4 shows two distinct relationships between entities and a beach scene and the scene and the objects themselves.

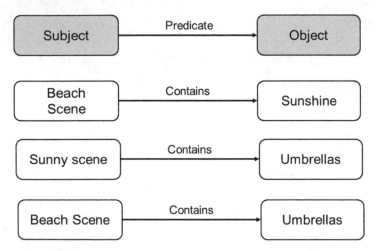

*Figure 4-4.*  *Representing contextual relationships*

These relationships can also be combined to present a combined view of scene-specific context as shown in Figure 4-5.

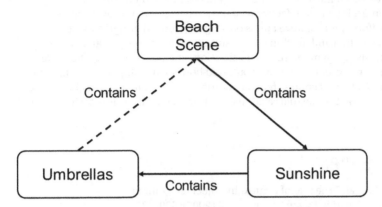

***Figure 4-5.*** *Deducing complex contextual relationship*

Of course, this is just one form of context representation and many other possible variations exist in research and implementations. Readers are referred to the references for more details on these.

Different contextual relationships have different strengths. For example, spatial relationships are not always strict (keyboard, monitor) vs. (firepost, ground). Generally, stronger relationship makes contextual recognition easier.

# 4.7   Concluding Thoughts on Scene Understanding

For scene understanding from images, the identity of underlying scenes can be gauged from the low-level aggregated feature statistics. State of the art methods in scene recognition are comprised of methods that represent the scene as a whole rather than splitting it into constituent scenes. These also form the basis for many contextual object recognition systems. Global representations have proven surprisingly effective for scene recognition.

## 4.7.1   Saliency vs Context for Recognition

When it comes to object detection, scene context has a bigger effect than the scene saliency. Context will direct the attention to relevant regions only while saliency will bring out the outliers. A scene composed of contextually related objects is more than just the sum of objects.

## 4.8   Summary

In this chapter we explored the role of context for effective recognition and understanding. Context is vital for effective recognition because it improves the application and platform performance and is one big step toward bridging the gap between human perception and machine understanding. Using context can make a difference between false recognition (or no recognition) and positive recognition. We discussed the ways to represent context and outlined how relationship representation is a building block toward efficient context representation and usage. In the next chapter we will focus on how to extract contextual relationships from scenes as well as techniques to represent relationships.

## 4.9   References

- Oliva, A. et al. "The role of context in object recognition." *Trends in Cognitive Sciences*, 11, no. 12 (2007): 520–527.

- Auckland, M.E. et al. "Non-target objects can influence perceptual processes during object recognition." *Psychon. Bull. Rev.* 14, no. 2 (2007): 332–337.

- Davenport, J.L. and M.C. Potter. "Scene consistency in object and background perception." *Psychol. Sci.* 15, no. 8 (2004): 559–564.

- Gordon, R.D. "Attentional allocation during the perception of scenes." *J. Exp. Psychol. Hum. Percept. Perform.* 30, no. 4 (2004): 760–777.

- Palmer, S.E. "The effects of contextual scenes on the identification of objects." *Mem. Cognit.* 3, no. 5 (1975): 519–526.

- Kunar, M.A. et al. "Does Contextual Cuing Guide the Deployment of Attention?" *J. Exp. Psychol. Hum. Percept. Perform.* 33, no. 4 (2007): 816–828.

# CHAPTER 5

■ ■ ■

# Extracting and Representing Relationships

The relationship extraction between different recognized entities defines the second level of operations in a knowledge pipeline after the recognition. While the recognition concentrates on identifying and labeling individual entities from the sensor data, relationships explicitly demonstrate the connections between the entities.

Chapter 4 showed some examples of how contextual relatinships manifest themselves in entities. Figure 5-1 below resembles Figure 4-4 and shows the subject-predicate-object relationship between the entities. The figure shows that the author and coffee are related by the fact that one entity (author) likes the other (coffee).

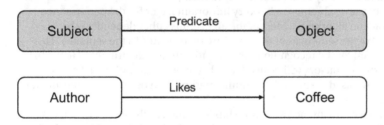

***Figure 5-1.*** *How context determines relationships*

To understand relationship extraction methods at a high level we will focus on text-based relationship extraction methods. The best way to understand relationship extraction is from text example, since many other modalities convert to text after recognition.

Further, many methods for direct relationship extraction from modes like video and speech are derived from text relationship extraction. We will show an example of extracting relationships from video.

© Omesh Tickoo and Ravi Iyer 2017
O. Tickoo and R. Iyer, *Making Sense of Sensors*, DOI 10.1007/978-1-4302-6593-1_5

# 5.1 High-level View of Extracting Relationships from Text

As discussed before, at its very basic level a relationship is what connects two (recognized) entities together. A first order relationship connects two entities through one predicate. Higher order relationships connect one or more entities by multiple predicates.

Figure 5-2 shows an example of a first order relationship. For an example of a higher order relationship, consider the problem of ordering food and wine at a restaurant. The relationship that can be used in this scenario would ideally connect a person's food preferences with the available choices along with the most suitable wine pairings.

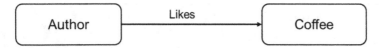

***Figure 5-2.*** *An example of a relationship*

For this chapter, we will mainly concentrate on extracting first order relationships. To understand the methods for text-based relationship extraction, we assume that the relationship is embedded in a sentence containing the entities and the description of the relationship is available (implicitly or explicitly) through the sentence. The methods to extract relationship rely on either using pretrained relationship structure information or learning the structure on the fly to unearth the relationships.

The structure of a textual sentence is a very important factor for the performance of the relation extraction algorithms. Most of the algorithms either depend on the syntactical meaning of the sentences or the structure of the words in the sentence. This makes it very important for the recognition methods to output well-structured text if the text-based relationship extractors will be used in subsequent stages. We will discuss an example of how video-based scene understanding methods can output such information later in this chapter.

More formally, given a sentence a relationship is defined as the tuple $t = (e\_1, e\_2, ..., e\_n)$ where $e\_i$ is an entity participating in a predefined relationship "r." The task of a relationship extractor can be broken down into the following parts:

- Identify the relevant entities in the relationship.

- Identify the role of each entity participating in the relationship.

As shown in Figure 5-3, for a textual relationship extraction task, this breaks down into an unstructured and a structured text analysis phase. During the unstructured text analysis phase the algorithm works on the sentence semantics to identify different grammatical and syntactical parts of the sentence. The structured phase usually starts with the identification of the participating entities in a relationship. This is followed by the relationship detection and result expression.

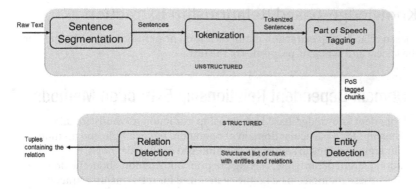

*Figure 5-3.*  *Unstructured and structured portions of relationship extraction*

# 5.2    Relationship Extraction Methods

The text-based relationship extraction methods can be broken down into different categories as shown in Figure 5-4.

- knowledge-based relationship extraction

- supervised relationship extraction

- semi-supervised relationship extraction

- distant supervision

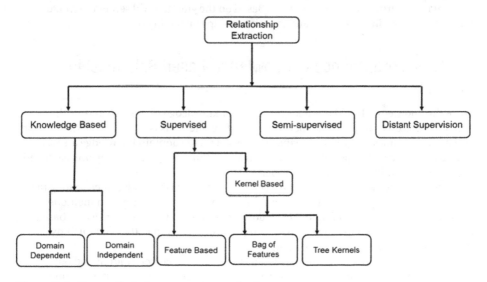

*Figure 5-4.*  *Types of relation extraction methods*

## 5.2.1   Knowledge-based Relationship Extraction

Knowledge-based relationship extraction methods rely on prior information of either the domain or the lexical and syntactic properties of the text.

### 5.2.1.1   Domain Dependent Relationship Extraction Methods

The domain dependent knowledge-based relationship extraction methods are tailored to extract relationships for a particular domain of operation. For example, the methods are tailored to find relationships in sentences pertaining to cancer diagnosis, fruit tree diseases, migration pattern of birds, etc. Having the prior information about the domain of operation allows these methods to be highly customized for relationship extraction. Using pre-existing information from the sentences for the given domain, the methods can achieve high accuracy, since the patterns for relationship expression in a given domain are usually quite regular and well known. In a specific application domain, usually there is a finite number of ways entities and their relationships can be expressed in text. This makes training the methods to extract them very accurate.

### 5.2.1.2   Domain Independent Relationship Extraction Methods

Also called lexico-syntactic pattern-based relationship extraction, these methods assume a set of patterns in the sentences that describe the relationships present in equivalent forms. The models extracting the relationships through this method are trained to recognize various sentence structures that represent the same relationship between entities in different but equivalent forms. The methods completely rely on the natural language and the syntactical structure of the sentences. Based on the grammatical sentence structures, the methods identify the entities and the relationship connecting them.

### 5.2.1.3   Performance of Knowledge-based Relationship methods

Since the knowledge-based methods rely on prior knowledge of domain and/or the language lexicon and syntax, the performance of the methods is highly dependent on the size of the training set representing the rules based on the domain knowledge and the language structure. The performance of such algorithms as represented by precision and recall metrics exhibit the following properties:

Precision measures the amount of relations that are correctly identified among the given set of sentences. Generally, the knowledge-based relation extraction methods exhibit a high degree of precision. This follows from the fact that the knowledge-based relation extraction methods are trained with examples that depict the relationships through unambiguous sentence structures.

Recall measures the amount of relationships that were correctly identified out of the total available relationships in a test set. Knowledge-based relation extraction methods usually score low on the recall metric. This follows from the fact that the training methods cannot cover all possible variations of the sentence structures for relationship expression. More often, the rules do not consider a majority of the structures expressing a relationship leading to misidentification of many relationships as false.

## 5.2.2 Supervised Relationship Extraction

Supervised relationship extraction methods rely on pretrained models to identify the named entities in a sentence and the task of relationship extraction is converted to one of classification. The supervised methods typically involve a preprocessing step that identifies the entities of interest and any connections between them. The connections are then processed through the classification methods to confirm predefined relationships as shown in Figure 5-5.

**Figure 5-5.** *Relationship extraction pipe*

At a high level the pipeline can be divided into the following parts based on the functionality.

- The preprocessing stage is responsible for detecting the entities that may be part of a relationship. All such possible entities are identified using the knowledge of sentence structures (syntax) and natural language properties (semantics). Using this information helps to isolate the entities that may be candidates for relationship subject or predicate and also parts of the sentences that may be key to discovering the presence of the relationship. For example, given a sentence "John said Andy Grove was one of the founders of Intel Corporation," the preprocessing step might identify the entities "John, Andy Grove, and Intel" as the entities that may be participating in a relationship described by the part or the whole of the subsentence "was one of the founders of." Given these identifications, the next block formats the entities and the sentence in a format based on the type of classification stage used.

- Classifiers are trained with both a positive and a negative set of training examples. The next subsections pages describe some of the popular methods for classification to extract relationships.

## 5.2.2.1 Feature-based Methods

Feature-based methods express the entities and the sentences describing relationships as set of features. These features are usually a combination of the semantic and syntactic features extracted from the text.

The syntactic features extracted include:

- entities

- types of entities

- subsentences that may describe the relationships between the entities

- number of entities and the number of words in the sentence

- number and the sequence of words potentially describing the relationship

Semantic features usually include the word paths between the entities.

For the training of the feature-based classifiers, multiple positive and negative example feature sets are generated from sentences representing known relationship structures. These feature sets are then used to train the classifiers for determining the presence or absence of a pretrained relationship. This consideration also makes it very hard to choose the right features, since some features may represent parts of the sentence that are good indicators of the underlying relationship expression while others may be representing bad indicators.

Feature-based methods completely rely on the human perception and labor at the training phase to identify as many positive and negative examples from text as possible. It is easy to notice, however, that such cases can lead to missing relationships in text that was not available at the training time. Since the language can represent a relationship in formats that span a large set, it is virtually impossible for feature-based training to cover all the possible cases.

## 5.2.2.2 Kernel-based Methods

Kernel-based methods aim to solve the issue of training seen with feature-based methods by using kernels that compare the similarity of the test sentences with the previously known examples. Instead of exactly matching the word sequences through features like the feature-based methods, the kernel-based methods try to extract the similarity to known representations instead of looking for more exact matches.

There are two main types of kernel-based relationship extraction methods: bag of features kernels and tree kernels

Bag of Features Kernels: The bag of features-based kernel method works by creating the representations of different parts of the sentence containing the entities.

Such methods are based on string properties and the actual functional kernels compute the similarity in the subsequences of learned and test images. The subsequences are divided and compared based on their position in the sentence relative to the entities being investigated. If the similar parts of the sentence are long and contiguous, the kernel-based methods will return a better match as compared to short, noncontiguous similar parts in sentences.

As an example, if e_1 and e_2 are the two entities of interest, the sentence containing them could be subdivided into a sequence s_1, e_1, s_2, e_2, and s_3 where

- s_1 is the part of the sentence before the first entity e_1;

- s_2 is the part of the sentence between entities e_1 and e_2;

- s_3 is the part of the sentence after the second entity e_2.

Given the sentence "The author of this book likes coffee as a breakfast drink," if the preprocessing step identifies "author" and "coffee" as the entities e_1 and e_2 respectively, the values of the other parameters would be

- s_1 is "The";

- s_2 is "of this book likes";

- s_3 is "as a breakfast drink."

The similarity score is calculated at the word level, i.e., the words themselves are converted into feature representations before applying a classifier.

Tree Kernels: As opposed to the bag of features-based methods, the tree kernels use the structure information from the sentence to determine the presence or absence of relationship between two entities identified in the preprocessing step. The structure includes the words and the order of the words in the sentences.

The methods construct a shallow parse tree for representing the sequence of words as well as the entities in a given sentence. The sentence "John said Andy Grove was one of the founders of Intel Corporation" can be represented in the tree form as shown in Figure 5-6.

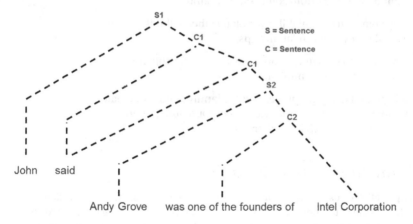

*Figure 5-6.* *Representing a sentence as a tree*

Assuming the preprocessing step identified the entities "John," "Andy Grove," and "Intel Corporation," the following parse trees are identified. Two sentences (subsentences) S1 and S2 containing the entities are represented as parse trees as shown in Figure 5-7. Of course, for this example S1 represents the complete input sentence.

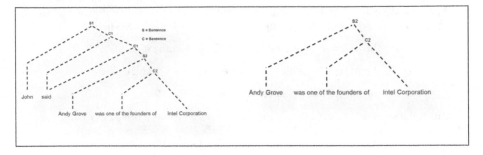

***Figure 5-7.*** *Possible parse trees for the sentence*

The tree S1 is not shallow since it is not the smallest tree containing the relationship ("founder") while S2 represents such a shallow tree. For the purpose of training, the sentence S1 is used as a negative example while S2 serves as the positive example.

While the structural information helps kernel-based methods to achieve much better performance as measured by the precision and recall metrics, the method does assume that the predicate (relationship expressing word) is placed between the entities in the sentences. While not universally true, this structural information has been shown to be right for the majority of the cases.

## 5.2.2.3   Limitations of Supervised Methods

While the kernel-based methods improve over their feature-based counterparts, the supervised methods still suffer from some issues, mainly

- they demonstrate scalability problems; the methods are hard to extend to cover new relationships;

- extensions to recognize more than one relationship from a sentence are hard to implement;

- the methods need preprocessing to identify entities or create parse trees. These methods can be computationally and algorithmically hard to implement.

## 5.2.3   Semi-supervised Methods

The supervised methods discussed so far rely on the labeled data to train the models needed for relationship extraction. In many cases, obtaining this training data proves to be the most time-consuming task and usually the models suffer in performance because of inadequate training. The labeling task is not just a problem of scale, it also involves cumbersome human effort.

Semi-supervised relationship extraction methods tend to overcome the limitations of effective labeling by automating the labeling portion of the classifier training. Since obtaining the labeled data is expensive, the semi-supervised methods bootstrap the creation of training data by setting up a tight loop between the data labeling and relationship extraction modules. Generally, a weak learner outputs relationship information that can be used as training data for the next stage.

Figure 5-8 and the following steps broadly outline a semi-supervised relationship extraction system.

- Seeding: The algorithms generally start with some example tuples expressing the relationship. These examples are referred to as "seeds."

- Pattern Induction: The seed examples are used to learn (induce) patterns between the entities that depict the relationship.

- Relationship Extraction: The patterns are used to extract the sentences that embed the given relationship.

- New Pattern Addition and Seed Extension: Based on the extracted sentences, new patterns are recognized and added to the seed set.

- Iteration: The process repeats with a new pattern induction step.

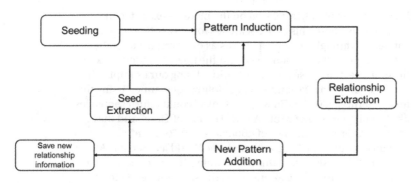

***Figure 5-8.*** *Semi-supervised relationship extraction flow*

We now show some examples of the process described above using popular semi-supervised relationship extraction methods.

## 5.2.3.1   Dual Iterative Pattern Relation Expansion (DIPRE)

Assume the relationship of interest is "book authors." In other words, we are interested in obtaining the relationship (author, publication) and extract as many such relationships as possible from a given set of documents. For the most popular text-based relation extraction tasks, the domain of search is the entire web. We will use the same for our example here.

- Seed Phase: Assuming that we seed the algorithm with a small sample of <author, book> relationships. The authors of the main paper used 5 relationship seeds.

- Entity Search Phase: The second phase involves searching for the tagged entities in the domain of interest. For the chosen seeds above, this would involve searching all the sentences that have the authors and the books appearing together. For our example, the search may return sentences containing the <author, book> pair connected through different sentence structures like "Isaac Asimov wrote The Robots of Dawn," "The author of The Robots of Dawn is Isaac Asimov," etc. Typically, large numbers of such sentences will be extracted by the search algorithms. In case of the authors of DIPRE the search resulted in close to 200 patterns being discovered using the 5 seeds used.

- New Pattern Generation Phase: Using the search results from the entity search phase, this phase examines each sentence to generate patterns that connect the entities together. For our example, the sentences returned above can lead to patterns of the form:"323076_1_En wrote <Book>" and "The author of <Book> is 323076_1_En" respectively.

- New Entity Search Phase: Based on the patterns extracted in the previous phase, this phase searches for new entities that are connected through the same patterns as discovered earlier. New entities replace the previous seed and the flow is handed back to the entity search phase for next iteration. Using our example, the patterns can yield new entities in the following manner. Using the first pattern, "323076_1_En wrote <Book>" could return sentences like "Stephen Hawking wrote A Brief History of Time" and the second pattern "The author of <Book> is 323076_1_En" can return sentences of the type "The author of The World as I See It is Albert Einstein." We observe that this step is able to expand the specific entities with the same relationship as the seed entities. One can now add <Stephen Hawking, A Brief History of Time> and <Albert Einstein, The World as I See It> to the seed list and repeat the process again to get more formats for relationship description and more entities sharing similar relationships.

- Termination Criteria: A termination criteria based on the number of extracted entities and relationship types is generally used to stop the execution. In our example, a specific number of <Author, Book> pair discoveries could be used as termination criteria.

Figure 5-9 shows the complete flow for the algorithm.

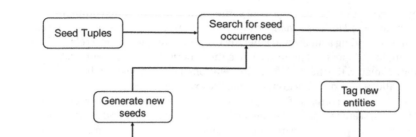

**Figure 5-9.** *DIPRE flow*

## 5.2.3.2   Snowball

DIPRE forms the foundation of many popular semi-supervised relationship extraction methods. A major drawback of the method employed by DIPRE concerns the use of exact phrases and word order in sentences to extract the entities in the New Entity Search Phase. Basically, the algorithm searches for exact matches of the word and order of these words in a sentence to extract the entities. As an example, the pattern "The author of <Book> is 323076_1_En" will return the sentence "The author of The World as I See It is Albert Einstein" but will fail to return the sentence "The author of the book The World as I See It is Albert Einstein" because the word "book" is not part of the original template.

To avoid such strict template matching, Snowball uses functionality similar to the kernel-based supervised relationship extraction methods. The patterns are broken down into multiple parts like the supervised methods. As in the supervised method, if e_1 and e_2 are the two entities of interest, the sentence (pattern) containing them could be subdivided into a sequence s_1 e_1 s_2 e_2 s_3 where

- s_1 is the part of the pattern before the first entity e_1;

- s_2 is the part of the pattern between entities e_1 and e_2;

- s_3 is the part of the pattern after the second entity e_2.

Snowball uses the same procedure flow as DIPRE except for one change. The New Entity Search Phase uses kernel-based similarity methods for the s_1, s_2, and s_3 parts of the pattern instead of an exact match. The similarity metric makes it possible to tag the sentences that are lexically and semantically similar to the target pattern without requiring an exact match.

The original Snowball algorithm was used to extract the <Organization, Location> relationship from the web data but the algorithm is generic enough to be used for any single order entity extraction task.

## 5.2.3.3    KnowItAll

Thus far all the methods discussed have used some form of user-provided domain-specific patterns as a seed for relationship extraction. KnowItAll systems attempt to relax this restriction by providing a method to label the training examples using a relatively small set of domain-independent patterns. Since the generic patterns are applicable across different domains, the method identifies relation-specific rules and then uses specific instantiations for extracting domain-specific extraction rules.

The KnowItAll system consists of multiple stages. The main blocks of operation are a bootstrapping unit, search engine, relationship extractor, an assessor, and a knowledge base. At the heart of the system is a search engine that uses the information from the web to return web pages based on queries from the bootstrapping unit and the extractor. In addition, the search engine provides the hit count from the search to aid in probability calculation for the importance of the search result. In general, a higher number of similar relationship expressions returned by the search engine points to a valid relationship extracted. The bootstrapping unit uses generic rule templates to form rules and information about the domain to focus the search. For example, "X such as Y" is a rule that implies a generic similarity between the entities X and Y and can be used to find domain-specific entities. Applying the constraint of searching for "cities" can combine with the rule above to search for relationships containing cities in statements like "cities such as New York."

The extractor unit applies the rules from the bootstrapping unit to the search results to extract the pages with statements that conform to the search. The extractions are then sent to the assessor, which thresholds the results based on the probability of occurrence (using hit count) before storing the final relationships results in a knowledge base. The assessor uses domain-specific discriminators provided by the bootstrapping unit by applying the information focus constraint (domain-specific) to the extracted results. Readers are referred to the references at the end of the chapter for a more thorough description of the KnowItAll system.

## 5.2.3.4    TextRunner

As compared with DIPRE, Snowball, and KnowItAll systems, the TextRunner system is designed to discover the relationships without any human input and train classifiers based on self-discovered positive and negative training examples. The purpose of the text runner system is to go through a given textual repository, search for relationship patterns, and train classifiers that can then be used to extract different relationships from new text sentences.

The method employs extractors and assessors like KnowItAll but replaces the bootstrapping methods with a domain-independent classifier training method.

The learning method takes a pool of documents as an input. The documents could be scrapped off the web or provided to the algorithm by other methods. The first step divides the sentence into chunks and identifies the entities (nouns) and possible predicates. Step 2 attempts to find possible relationships between the entities. Steps 3, 4, and 5 use different parsing techniques (syntactic, dependency, and pre-constrained) to filter out the identified relationships as positive or negative examples of relationships. Step 6 trains a classifier using the positive and negative examples generated. Many types of classifiers have been employed by the authors. Readers are referred to the reference section of this chapter for a detailed description of the system.

# 5.3   NEIL (Never Ending Image Learning)

So far we concentrated on relationship extraction from text-based input. The methods discussed form the foundation of relationship extraction from data generated through various sensing modalities. NEIL attempts to use the methods outlined above to detect and extract relationships from images. The algorithm operates as outlined below.

- -Candidate entity detector training: The algorithm uses different ways to seed the process of visual relationship extraction from text. The first step is to perform the entity detection. Entities in this case are defined as objects, object attributes, and scenes. The image seeds can be provided manually along with the annotations for training. A more efficient way, however, is to use the text-based image search (inventors used Google image search) to retrieve large amount of images for each entity search. Multiple detectors are trained on each entity over the retrieved images. For example, we could train tens or hundreds of classifiers to detect a bicycle. Having multiple detectors solves the problems of overfitting (having the model detect only one kind/shape of bicycle) and coverage for high dimensionality of objects, scenes, and attributes (e.g., "cars" come in many shapes, sizes, and colors and a "car" detector must be able to detect a majority of these). Consensus on multiple detectors for an entity is then used to decide on the detection result.

- Relationship Discovery: After the entity detector detects the entities (objects, attributes, and scenes), the relationship discovery step attempts to find the following type of relationships:

- Object-object relationships: The object-object relationship discovery comprises of finding out the partonomic, taxonomic, and similarity relationship between the objects. Partonomic relationships describe if one object is a part of another (nose is a part of the face), taxonomic relationships connect the instances to broader classes (iPhone is a mobile phone), and the similarity relationships discover objects that are similar to each other (bees look similar to wasps). The object-object relationship discovery is performed through the use of object bounding boxes. The detectors identify the objects in an image and "draw" bounding boxes around them. Depending on the relative position of these bounding boxes, the relationship discovery stage can identify the inter-object relationships. For example, one bounding box nested in another indicates a partonomic relationship. Two different detectors bounding the same object in multiple images indicates taxonomic and similarity relationships. Object bounding boxes that occur close to each other consistently can indicate a spatial relationship (monitor is consistently close to a keyboard in images).

- Object-attribute relationships: Object detectors and attribute detectors firing consistently together can indicate a strong object-attribute relationship. "Sun is bright" and "ball is spherical" are some examples of object-attribute relationships.

- Scene-object relationship: In a manner similar to object-attribute relationship, the scene-object relationship attempts to find the objects that occur consistently in certain scenes. For example, "ships are found in the ocean."

- Scene-attribute relationship: The scene-attribute relationships discovered include relationships of the type "park is green," "night is dark," etc.

- New Instance Discovery: Using the relationships found in the previous step, the algorithm tries to find new instances of entities. For example, sometime the detectors may fail to detect a certain instance of an entity (a non-trained instance or type of a car) but using the discovered relationships can make it easy to detect these new instances (shapes, color, scene, etc. that cars are most associated with can point to an object likely being a car).

- Retraining of detectors: Using the newly discovered instances, the detectors are retrained and the process of entity discovery starts afresh.

As the name suggests, Never Ending Image Learning is a continuous iterative process that works to increase the relationships discovered in an infinite loop through the steps described above.

## 5.4 Summary

This concludes the chapter on relationship discovery. In this chapter we discussed how major relationship extraction methods are based on textual relationship discovery. We discussed the knowledge-based relationship extraction methods including domain-dependent and domain-independent methods. Supervised textual relationship extraction methods include feature- and kernel-based methods. To reduce human labeling costs for training, semi-supervised methods attempt to automatically label the seed relationships and entities through iterative methods starting with manual or auto-generated seeds. With NEIL as an example, we discussed how text-based relationship extraction concepts directly extend to relationship extraction in other sensing domains. The next chapter outlines the methods to use the relationship information to build knowledge bases and operate on discovered relationships for different usages.

# 5.5 References

- Agichtein, E., & Gravano, L. (2000). Snowball: Extracting relations from large plain-text collections. Proceedings of the Fifth ACM International Conference on Digital Libraries.

- Banko, M., Cafarella, M. J., Soderland, S., Broadhead, M., & Etzioni, O. (2007). Open information extraction from the web. IJCAI '07: Proceedings of the 20th International Joint Conference on Artificial Intelligence. Hyderabad, India.

- Brin, S. (1998). Extracting patterns and relations from the world wide web. WebDB Workshop at 6th International Conference on Extending Database Technology, EDBT '98.

- Bunescu, R. C., & Mooney, R. J. (2005a). A shortest path dependency kernel for relation extraction. HLT '05: Proceedings of the conference on Human Language Technology and Empirical Methods in Natural Language Processing (pp. 724–731). Vancouver, British Columbia, Canada: Association for Computational Linguistics.

- Bunescu, R. C., & Mooney, R. J. (2005b). Subsequence kernels for relation extraction. Neural Information Processing Systems, NIPS 2005, Vancouver, British Columbia, Canada.

- Culotta, A., McCallum, A., & Betz, J. (2006). Integrating probabilistic extraction models and data mining to discover relations and patterns in text. Proceedings of the main conference on Human Language Technology Conference of the North American Chapter of the Association of Computational Linguistics (pp. 296–303). New York, New York: Association for Computational Linguistics.

- Culotta, A., & Sorensen, J. (2004). Dependency tree kernels for relation extraction. ACL '04: Proceedings of the 42nd Annual Meeting on Association for Computational Linguistics (p. 423). Morristown, NJ, USA: Association for Computational Linguistics.

- Etzioni, O., Cafarella, M., Downey, D., Popescu, A. M., Shaked, T., Soderland, S., Weld, D. S., & Yates, A. (2005). Unsupervised Named-Entity Extraction from the Web: An Experimental Study. Artificial Intelligence (pp. 191–134).

- GuoDong, Z., Jian, S., Jie, Z.,&Min, Z. (2002). Exploring various knowledge in relation extraction. Proceedings of the 43rd Annual Meeting on Association for Computational Linguistics (pp. 419– 444).

- Kambhatla, N. (2004). Combining lexical, syntactic, and semantic features with maximum entropy models for extracting relations. Proceedings of the ACL 2004.

- Liu,Y., Shi, Z.,&Sarkar, A. (2007). Exploiting rich syntactic information for relationship extraction from biomedical articles. Human Language Technologies 2007: The Conference of the North American Chapter of the Association for Computational Linguistics; Companion Volume, Short Papers (pp. 97–100). Rochester, New York: Association for Computational Linguistics.

- Lodhi, H., Saunders, C., Shawe-Taylor, J., & Cristianini, N. (2002). Text classification using string kernels. Journal of Machine Learning Research (pp. 419–444).

- McDonald, R. (2004). Extracting relations from unstructured text. UPenn CIS Technical Report.

- Zelenko, D., Aone, C., & Richardella, A. (2003). Kernel methods for relation extraction. Journal of Machine Learning Research.

- Zhao, S., & Grishman, R. (2005). Extracting relations with integrated information using kernel methods. Proceedings of the 43rd Annual Meeting on Association for Computational Linguistics (pp. 419–426).

# CHAPTER 6

■ ■ ■

# Knowledge and Ontologies

So far the chapters in the book have focused on the primary task of data acquisition and relationship extraction. For the more sophisticated applications, specifically the ones that exhibit some form of intelligence, the relationship information forms the basis of reasoning and interpretation. The recent surge in Artificial Intelligence (AI) applications and other data analytics-based services is in part because of technologies taking advantage of the various knowledge representation mechanisms. In this chapter we focus on introducing some of the popular methods for knowledge representation and their usages.

As we discussed in the previous chapter, a relationship between entities in its simplest forms can be expressed as a triplet with the relationship connecting an object with a subject. We reproduce here in Figure 6-1, a figure we used to illustrate this concept earlier in the book.

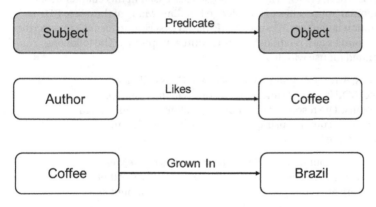

***Figure 6-1.*** *Relationship triples*

A few methods to extract these types of relationships were discussed in the previous chapter. We also briefly discussed how multiple triplets with common elements (object or subject) can be combined to form extensions of relationships, commonly termed as knowledge as depicted in Figure 6-2.

O. Tickoo and R. Iyer, *Making Sense of Sensors*, DOI 10.1007/978-1-4302-6593-1_6

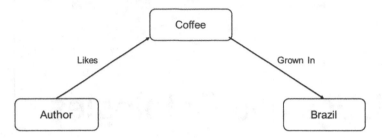

***Figure 6-2.*** *First steps from relationship to knowledge*

These methods form the foundation of knowledge building. Repeating this basic step results in a graph of knowledge that embeds the relationships already discovered through relationship extraction and provides the too to identify the new relationships emerging from the graph structure itself.

This graph is generally supplemented with tools that can perform logical operations on the graph to reason and interpret the current relationship structure and infer new relationships based on this knowledge from the graph.

# 6.1   Relationship Representation using RDF

Relationship Description Format (RDF) is the format for describing semantic relationships between entities. The format has been adopted as a recommendation by the World Wide Web consortium (W3C). The technologies discussed in this chapter describe some of the most popular approaches to knowledge building. Many of these use RDF as the semantic description language. RDF uses XML-based description formats to describe various entities as resources and relationships as resource properties. The following components are defined for use with RDF:

- Resources: Any entity that is described by RDF is called a resource. RDF is very flexible when it comes to the resource descriptions. The resources are generally defined and referred to as part of a "document" using a standard XML-based format as shown in Figure 6-2.

- Properties: Attributes of entities are described as properties in the RDF document. The relationships of resources with other resources are also embedded in the description document as a property.

- Statements: An RDF statement is defined as a collection of an RDF resource along with one or more attributes plus the properties associated with those attributes. At its very basic form, the RDF statement represents an entity with its relationships to other entities. A complete knowledge-based graph is a collection of such statements.

RDF makes it very easy to construct knowledge-based graphs. It adds flexibility to the knowledge generation and representation process. New attributes can be added to resources by updating the XML statements. Similarly, new relationships are added by simple document update.

Source: `http://www.w3schools.com/xml/xml:rdf.asp`

Figure 6-3 shows an example RDF document. The document refers to the resource "`http://www.w3school.com`" and the document contains two attributes (title, author). The attributes point to relationships with other resources. Figure 6-4 shows the graphical representation of the relationship described by the document in Figure 6-3.

```
<?xml version="1.0"?>

<rdf:RDF
xmlns:rdf="http://www.w3.org/1999/02/22-rdf-syntax-ns#"
xmlns:si="http://www.w3schools.com/rdf/">

<rdf:Description rdf:about="http://www.w3schools.com">
  <si:title>W3Schools</si:title>
  <si:author>Jan Egil Refsnes</si:author>
</rdf:Description>

</rdf:RDF>
```

**Figure 6-3.** *RDF document*

**Figure 6-4.** *Relationship described by the RDF document for Figure 6-3*

# 6.2   Freebase: Database of Relationships

Freebase was one of the first relationship-based data stores. It was started by a company called Metaweb that aimed to provide a relationship-based database access to commercial and non-commercial organizations. The database was built up on user-submitted triplets as well as the relationships discovered from the web. The relationship information contribution to the database was designed to be completely collaborative, with anyone having the ability to submit relationship triplets for consideration to be included as part of the database. Triplets used the RDF format for description. At its peak, Freebase contained about 1.9 billion triplets depicting relationships. The company was acquired by Google is 2010 and the database was used to partly construct Google's Knowledge Graph. The sketch in Figure 6-5 shows an equivalent representation of a knowledge store similar to FreeBase-based graphs.

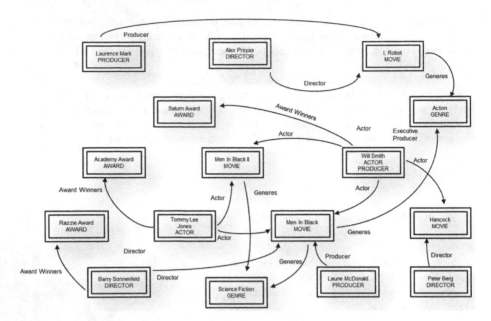

***Figure 6-5.*** *An example rendition similar to a FreeBase knowledge store*

# 6.3 ConceptNet: Common Sense Knowledge

ConceptNet is an initiative from MIT (http://alumni.media.mit.edu/~hugo/
publications/papers/BTTJ-ConceptNet.pdf) that attempts to represent and provide
access to common sense knowledge. Concepts like "A lemon is sour," "Fire is hot,"
and "To open a door one must usually turn a knob" are common sense concepts that
humans understand but computers need to be told. Having a knowledge base for such
concepts can significantly aid the machine understanding of higher-level concepts. For
example, asking a robot to "Go outside" implicitly assumes opening a door by turning
a knob. ConceptNet aims to provide this common sense in the form of a knowledge
base containing a massive amount of common sense information. Figure 6-6 shows an
example of how ConceptNet might represent and store common sense knowledge.

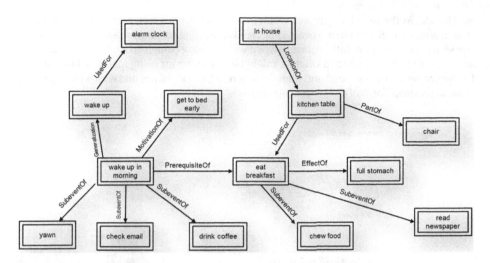

***Figure 6-6.*** *A sketch representing part of ConceptNet for common sense knowledge*

# 6.4   Microsoft's Satori

Microsoft is actively building a knowledge representation repository called Microsoft Satori. Currently the repository contains more than a billion objects and relationships collected over multiple years. The main source of the knowledge is web data obtained using crawlers like the ones used by the search engine Bing. Similar to Google's Knowledge Graph, the aim of Satori is to understand the user requirements and provide intelligent assistance based on understanding of entity relationships. Satori utilizes sources like Freebase and Wikipedia to build the knowledge base. Like NEIL, the approach to knowledge building is automatic and the engine keeps running off a farm of servers (50,000+) to find new relationships and analyze the existing knowledge for new connections.

Since the main target vehicle for Satori for usages is Bing, Microsoft is targeting the initial usages for recommendations by the browser. For example, the browser uses Satori for exploring different relationships to suggest possible vacation itineraries as well as things to do in different places to the users. Currently the browser offers "at-a-glance" answers and "snapshots" about the people, places, and things in search results. It also "auto-suggests" as users type to help disambiguate queries and get to answers more quickly.

The process involves understanding the general concepts as described by common sense and integrating that with domain-specific instantiations and relationships.

# 6.5   Google's Knowledge Graph

Google has made it public that it intends to provide a semantic search capability that exploits the relationships in the different forms from web pages. The data for these relationships can come from text, images, and video. Leveraging their cache of web data, Google has created a large knowledge graph from products like Maps, Finance, Movies and Music. As the search engine crawls for new data, the search engine returns data that is analyzed for inclusion in the ever-going rich knowledge graph. We can experience the semantic search operation at work when we are using Google to look for something and it tries to first understand what we might be searching for using machine learning (autocomplete, Google Next) and then returns results that are not just web pages but a human readable form of an answer (Figure 6-7).

***Figure 6-7.*** *Google understands a user query and responds with answers vs. webpage pointer (www.google.com)*

# 6.6   Wolfram Alpha

Wolfram Alpha is a knowledge engine with a search API built completely for answering queries with semantic responses. Unlike other commercial search engines that have started utilizing the data they have for generating knowledge, Wolfram Alpha was designed with the goal of generating knowledge from web resources and providing both commercial and non-commercial users access to this data for their applications. The result is a web tool that actually answers user's questions by traversing the knowledge-based graph it has built (Figure 6-8).

*Figure 6-8. Wolfram Alpha query example (`https://www.wolframalpha.com/`)*

Total data stored by Wolfram Alpha's knowledge engine currently exceeds 10 trillion entities and relationships. The number of algorithms and models used to work on the data exceeds 50,000.

The search engine works continuously in the background to discover new data and relationships. It currently can answer your questions, teach you music, compare books, and give you semantic weather information. Wolfram Alpha's engine has been integrated with many popular search engines.

# 6.7  Facebook's Entity Graph

Similar to Google, Facebook has a lot of data provided by the users as part of their profile and interactions using the social network. Facebook's Entity Graph is based on this information. During its initial days, the company used to keep user information as a simple text-based data store. In recent times, it has realized the power of relating the data to each other and has switched from plain text representation to a structured representation of the user's social data. Having the ability to represent the user information and various social relationships in a knowledge-based graph (called Entity Graph by Facebook) enables the company to provide rich services to the users by suggesting new connections based on existing social connections and user preferences. The Entity Graph is also used for providing contextual search results on the social networking site. For example, when you search for a name on Facebook, the site operates on the structured data provided by the Entity Graph and the results returned are ranked according to the best fit for you based on your social connections and activity.

# 6.8 Apple's Siri

Apple's widely popular personal assistant Siri is built on the semantic search abilities provided by engines like Wolfram Alpha.

# 6.9 Semantic Web

We end this chapter with a very brief introduction to the concepts of the semantic web. Currently, most of the World Wide Web is a syntactical collection of documents, i.e., the web pages express concepts and ideas that stand fairly independently from other ideas on other web pages. Of course, the syntax allows for explicit hyperlinking of entities between the web pages.

This kind of syntactical structure is easy for humans to understand, but the evolution of intelligent machines raises the need for a web that can be understood by the machines as well. Humans can parse the syntactical web effectively because the concepts of definitions and descriptions are inherently understood by us. A statement like "the cat jumped over a chair" makes sense to a human because we know what "cat," "jump," and "chair" mean. A machine parsing such a sentence, however, needs to know these concepts before it can make sense of the relationship between the entities in the sentence <cat, jumped over, chair>. The current syntactic web is a collection of documents where the computers do the presentation and the humans provide the links between the information. The primary aim is the consumption of information by the humans. Unique identities on the web are reserved for the documents in the form of URLs (Universal Resource Locators), also called web addresses, like `www.intel.com`.

Current syntactical web layout makes it extremely difficult to process queries requiring background knowledge of the context, locate information that needs to combine multiple sources, reason about information from different web pages, etc. The root of the problem with the syntactical web is that all the embedded metadata in the web pages concentrates on the display properties only (font, placement, etc.) and none of the relationship information to other entities on the web is available for interpretation.

The semantic web is an attempt to make the web machine readable by providing access to information that can aid in making semantic sense of the web content. The start of this effort has been made by adding semantic annotations to the already existing content on the web. Before any such annotation can be used to describe concepts, it is important to agree on the "meanings" of the concepts and objects being described. This is done on the semantic web through the use of ontologies.

## 6.9.1 Ontologies

Ontologies in their basic form provide meanings for the terms. Meanings of the terms in ontologies is formally specified and made available to the users. New terms can be formed by combining the information on existing terms from the same or multiple ontologies. For the example above, an ontology could hold the definition of the "cat" being a four-legged animal and the "chair" being a four-legged piece of furniture. Animal and furniture could be further defined and described as part of an ontology.

Thus, the ontology for the semantic web is a vocabulary of terms to describe certain realities along with any assumptions regarding the meaning of these descriptions.

## 6.9.1.1 Components of an Ontology

Ontologies are comprised of two components

- Concept Names: Concept names describe terms. For example:

- Cat is a concept whose members are a kind of animal.

- Carnivore is a concept whose members are animals that eat parts of other animals.

- Background Knowledge: Background knowledge imparts meaning to terms. For example:

- Cats are carnivores.

- No individual can be both a carnivore and an herbivore.

## 6.9.1.2 Ontology Languages

For the semantic web, various attempts have been made to define suitable ontology languages. Prominent among them are RDFS and OWL. Since we focused on RDF as the resource description format for relationships earlier in this chapter, we will use RDFS as the means to understand ontologies.

RDFS or RDF Schema is intended to provide a vocabulary for terms used in RDF descriptions for the semantic web. RDFS is object-oriented in the sense that it groups the definitions and descriptions into multiple classes and their properties. The classes can have sub- and super- classes and the properties can define a range of applicable values.

RDFS schemas are pointed to by Universal Resource Identifiers or URIs. For the example of the relationship in the Figure 6-9, concepts/resources "Author," "likes," and "coffee" will be described by the RDFS at the descriptions stored at accessible web addresses referred to by URIs. Resources in general are any objects that can be referred to through URIs. Properties are also defined as resources.

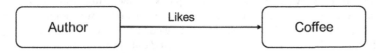

***Figure 6-9.*** *Basic relationship triple*

Figure 6-10 repeats the document presented in Figure 6-3 for us to observe the syntax for resource description.

```
<?xml version="1.0"?>

<rdf:RDF
xmlns:rdf="http://www.w3.org/1999/02/22-rdf-syntax-ns#"
xmlns:si="http://www.w3schools.com/rdf/">

<rdf:Description rdf:about="http://www.w3schools.com">
  <si:title>W3Schools</si:title>
  <si:author>Jan Egil Refsnes</si:author>
</rdf:Description>

</rdf:RDF>
```

***Figure 6-10.*** *RDF with RDFS embedding*

In the figure we see a statement "<rdf:Description rdf:about=http://www.w3schools.com">" pointing the parsing agent to the URI at http://www.w3schools.com for a description of resources "title" and "author."

Having the ability to link the instances and resource descriptions back to the common ontologies allows the computer programs to understand the knowledge representation and descriptions across different invocations. A cat can be interpreted as the same animal when referred to by the animal name "cat" or the pet name of an individual cat "Garfield." Ontological methods lend syntax to the web, allowing for expression of ideas vs. semantic document storage.

While RDFS is one way to implement ontologies, many other methods exist and each comes with a package/tool for computers to browse and make connections between concepts. First Order Logic (FOL)-based tools allow for combinations of concepts and generation of new ones. Ontology based on Ontology Web Language OWL (https://www.w3.org/OWL/) is one of the most popular ontologies accepted by the World Wide Web consortium. The OWL language comes with tools for people to build their own ontologies as well as operate on those already existing.

# 6.10   Summary

This chapter provided a brief overview of the ultimate step in knowledge understanding from sensor information. We introduced the concept of knowledge and how it can be viewed as a collection of semantic relationships. Many knowledge-based commercial applications were discussed that are heavily using the collected data from humans and the web to build knowledge repositories with an aim to provide intelligent services. The semantic web is the ultimate step in evolution of knowledge from raw data gathered by sensors. It is also the last step in our journey of knowledge from sensors. The topic of ontologies and the semantic web is large and fit for discussion in a dedicated book of its own. We hope to have given you a brief introduction to the topic and the resources in the reference section to follow the topic on your own. Interested readers can learn a lot more about the technologies discussed with the help of references at the end of this chapter. The next chapter will focus on the practical system and platform considerations to implement a sensor-understanding pipeline in the real world.

# 6.11    References

- Google Knowledge Graph https://www.google.com/intl/es419/insidesearch/features/search/knowledge.html

- ConceptNet http://alumni.media.mit.edu/~hugo/publications/papers/BTTJ-ConceptNet.pdf

- Wolfram Alpha Source: https://www.wolframalpha.com/

- Google Search www.google.com

- Ontology Web Language OWL (https://www.w3.org/OWL/)

- De Raedt, L, *Logical and Relational Learning*. Springer, 2008.

- Suchanek, F. M., Kasneci, G., and G. Weikum. "Yago: A Core of Semantic Knowledge" Proceedings of the 16th International Conference on World Wide Web.

- Carlson, J., Betteridge, B., Kisiel, B., Settles, E. R. H. Jr. and T. M. Mitchell. "Toward an Architecture for Never-Ending Language Learning." *Proceedings of the Twenty-Fourth Conference on Artificial Intelligence* (2010): 1306–1313.

- Bollacker, K., Evans, C., Paritosh, P., Sturge, T. and J. Taylor. "Freebase: A Collaboratively Created Graph Database for Structuring Human Knowledge." *Proceedings of the 2008 ACM SIGMOD International Conference on Management of Data.* (2008): 1247–1250.

- Singhal, A. "Introducing the Knowledge Graph: Things, Not Strings," May 2012. http://googleblog.blogspot.com/2012/05/introducing-knowledge-graph-things-not.html

- Weikum, G. and M. Theobald. "From Information to Knowledge: Harvesting Entities and Relationships from Web Sources." *Proceedings of the Twenty-ninth ACM SIGMOD-SIGACT-SIGART Symposium on Principles of Database Systems.* (2010): pp. 65–76.

- Davis, R., Shrobe, H., and P. Szolovits. "What is a Knowledge Representation?" *AI Magazine*, 14, no. 1, (1993): 17–33.

- Sowa, J. F. "Semantic Networks." *Encyclopedia of Cognitive Science*, 2006.

- Minsky, M. "A Framework for Representing Knowledge." *MIT-AI Laboratory Memo* (1974): 306.

- Berners-Lee, T. , Hendler, J. and O. Lassila, "The Semantic Web." 2001. http://www.scientificamerican.com/article/the-semantic-web

- Klyne, G. and J. J. Carroll, "Resource Description Framework (RDF): Concepts and Abstract Syntax." Feb. 2004. `http://www.w3.org/TR/2004/REC-rdf-concepts-20040210/`

- Cyganiak, R., Wood, D. and M. Lanthaler, "RDF 1.1 Concepts and Abstract Syntax." Feb. 2014. `http://www.w3.org/TR/2014/REC-rdf11-concepts-20140225/`

- Brachman, R. and H. Levesque, *Knowledge Representation and Reasoning*. San Francisco, CA, USA: Morgan Kaufmann Publishers Inc., 2004.

- West, R., Gabrilovich, E., Murphy, K., Sun, S., Gupta, R. and D. Lin. "Knowledge Base Completion via Search-based Question Answering." *Proceedings of the 23rd International Conference on World Wide Web*, (2014): 515–526.

- Lenat, D. B. "CYC: A Large-scale Investment in Knowledge Infrastructure." *Commun. ACM* 38, no. 11 (1995): 33–38.

- Vrandecic, D. and M. Krötzsch, "Wikidata: A Free Collaborative Knowledgebase." *Communications of the ACM* 57, no. 10, (2014): 78–85.

- Fader, A., Soderland, S. and O. Etzioni. "Identifying Relations for Open Information Extraction." *Proceedings of the Conference on Empirical Methods in Natural Language Processing.* (2011): 1535–1545.

- Qian, R. "Understand Your World with Bing, Bing Search Blog." Mar. 2013. `http://blogs.bing.com/search/2013/03/21/understand-your-world-with-bing/`

- Ferrucci, D., Brown, E., Chu-Carroll, J., Fan, J., Gondek, D., Kalyanpur, A. A., Lally, A., Murdock, J. W., Nyberg, E., Prager, J. and others, "Building Watson: An Overview of the DeepQA Project." *AI Magazine* 31, no. 3, (2010): 59–79.

# CHAPTER 7

■ ■ ■

# End-to-End System Architecture Implications

In this last chapter of the book, we discuss the system-level implications for processing sensor data and analyzing the processed data for insights and knowledge management. To get started, let's start by looking at what a typical end-to-end system architecture might look like. Figure 7-1 shows a few typical end-to-end system architectures for different environments consisting of three platforms.

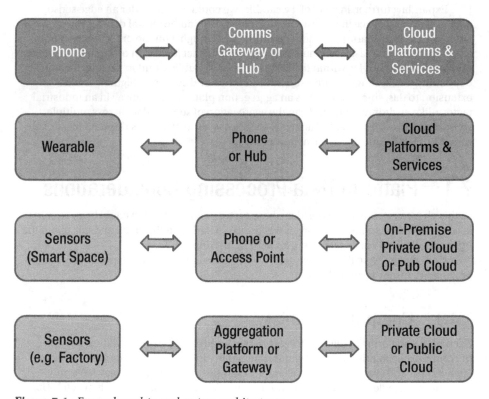

*Figure 7-1.* *Example end-to-end system architectures*

© Omesh Tickoo and Ravi Iyer 2017

O. Tickoo and R. Iyer, *Making Sense of Sensors*, DOI 10.1007/978-1-4302-6593-1_7

In Figure 7-1, the first end-to-end system architecture considers the phone as a sensor capture device. Today's phones capture valuable sensor data that includes location data (for navigation as well as assistance), audio data (speech Q&A), motion data (for health/fitness and navigation), and visual data (pictures and video for personal usage, social media, and other purposes). When such data is captured in a home environment, it goes through a communications gateway (for Wi-Fi communication) or a personal hub, and then becomes available to the cloud. While the gateway/hub is primarily used as a communication medium, such platforms have larger compute capabilities and could be used for additional local processing in some scenarios. Ultimately, the cloud platform is typically in a datacenter and has abundant processing resources available for analyzing the data as well as providing valuable services as a result of it.

Similarly, Figure 7-1 also shows a wearable example. Consider a fitness device on the wrist that measures your motion. Such a device typically has low bandwidth connectivity within a short range and therefore communicates to an on-body device like a phone for the ability to upload the data to the cloud when required. More sophisticated smart watch devices may have additional communication capabilities like Wi-Fi and cellular enabling them to also connect to a local connectivity hub as well as directly communicate with the cloud platform when required. The wearable typically has low compute capabilities for low power (mW to 100s mWs), whereas the phone or hub has high compute capabilities at medium power (Watts) and the cloud platform has the ability to scale to 10s/100s of Watts and beyond.

Expanding further, instead of a wearable, we could also consider an edge sensor device in a smart space that senses motion or captures audio/visual data for interactivity. Such devices in a smart space may communicate through a phone or local access point to the cloud. In this case, the cloud platform could in fact just be an on-premise platform that provides the service within the local vicinity or a public cloud in a datacenter depending on the usage of interest. The last end-to-end system in Figure 7-1 is an extension to this, since it considers an aggregation platform or gateway in an industrial factory-like environment to perform the aggregation of sensing data across multiple sensors and provides potential analytics locally as well as transmits this data to a private or public cloud platform for further processing.

# 7.1 Platform Data Processing Considerations

In this chapter, we will now consider where such sensor processing could be or should be accomplished for some of the usages we discussed earlier in this book and talk about the opportunities and challenges going forward in this domain.

Here are the typical considerations when determining where the processing should be done in an end-to-end platform:

## 7.1.1 Compute Capability

Each of the platforms in the end-to-end system architecture has very different levels of compute capabilities due to limitations in battery life, form factor, or other aspects such as cost and even cooling. For example, a simplistic sensor node may have only one microcontroller core and some simple control logic running at less than 100 MHz, whereas a gateway platform could have cores running at 100s of MHz to 1GHz as well as additional hardware logic for specialized media or communications functionality. The cloud platform typically has many cores, each running at multiple GHz. Given this wide possible range of compute characteristics, it becomes important to determine where to run parts of the overall application or service of interest. A sensor node, for example, may only be able to accomplish a little amount of processing, while sending the data to the gateway or cloud can enable much richer analytics and services.

## 7.1.2    Battery Life & Power Constraints

Typically, the reason behind the limited compute power available at a sensor node or a phone is the fact that it is battery-operated and therefore is required to run at milliwatts or several 10s of milliwatts on average. Given this characteristic, such devices are typically "asleep" for long periods of time and only do processing when some interesting sensor data arrives or an event of interest occurs. When considering speech processing, for instance, an edge device may only be able to determine whether there was a keyword spoken, whereas the actual command is processed on the gateway and the full Q&A processing and service is provided from the cloud. This is done in order to save the battery life and limit the cost of the sensor node.

## 7.1.3    Interactivity and Latency

The example provided above on speech recognition provides an interesting perspective in terms of partitioning of the overall workload. If interactivity and latency are important, one would like to run as much of the processing closer to the device as possible to minimize the latency of sending data to the cloud and getting back an answer. However, at the same time, interactivity may require access to data in the cloud where the domain expertise for generating the answer is actually available. One way of solving this problem is to consider local (user and device-specific) commands/questions vs. global commands/questions and enable local commands at the edge node (or nearby), while processing global (more generic) commands in the cloud.

- Bandwidth Availability

In addition to needing local processing for interactivity, the other key consideration for local processing is bandwidth availability. If the bandwidth available on the local node is very low, it becomes difficult (higher latency) to send all of the data to the cloud for processing. Communications processing also costs power and therefore there is typically a tradeoff between local compute vs. communication to the cloud. If the edge device is mobile, the availability of bandwidth also changes, depending on coverage at the current location as well as indoor vs. outdoor scenarios.

## 7.1.4    Storage & Memory Constraints

Due to form factor and power constraints, the amount of storage and memory available is also limited on a local edge device and grows as gateways and cloud platforms are considered. Therefore, if history is required for answering a question (speech example again), then it is almost imperative that the gateway or cloud provide the answer by processing the history in the context of the question. However, if the answer requires minimal history (only recent few seconds or minutes), then perhaps the local device has the ability to store the raw data or the metadata needed to answer questions later. In addition to historical data, having access to other data can also be equally important as discussed below.

## 7.1.5 Access to other data (crowd-sourced or expert data)

Access to data from other devices or previously collected data may also be useful when doing a Q&A session (speech example). Therefore, the cloud platforms have an advantage in performing the Q&A that requires data for specific domains. If the data is crowdsourced, the approach could be hierarchical where the local gateways can provide some context but the ultimate root of the hierarchy is the cloud platform where all crowdsourced data can be aggregated, processed, and stored.

## 7.1.6 Throughput & Batch processing

In some cases, the analytics requires a large amount of data to be collected and processed together. For example, if there is a transcription on an event required and this transcription is not required to be real-time, then processing at the cloud is more suitable than at the edge. The availability of the entire data can help better analytics in terms of summarizing the event as well as better context for various sections of the transcription. Such scenarios tend to be biased towards cloud execution rather than local execution on the edge device.

## 7.1.7 Security and Privacy

Privacy plays an important role in determining local vs. cloud processing. If the data is sensitive, then the bias towards local processing is high due to considerations such as loss of data integrity and exposure of the data, as well as concern over security breaches. In addition to local processing on the edge device, the consideration for on-premise servers vs. public cloud infrastructure is also dependent on the sensitivity of the data and the availability of security capabilities to anonymize the data as well as protect it from being misused.

## 7.1.8 Hierarchical processing

Ultimately, the benefits and trade-offs between local edge device processing and cloud processing end up with a convergence towards hierarchical processing, where some processing is done on the edge and the amount of processing accomplished at the gateway and the cloud progressively increases. The use of hierarchy is not limited only to basic static partitioning but also dynamic approaches that exploit the availability of many distributed nodes to perform the processing in a parallel manner.

## 7.2    End-to-end System Partitioning and Architecture

Figure 7-2 illustrates the above considerations for partitioning the workload between the three platforms in the end-to-end architecture. The figure shows how the considerations above bias the location of data processing between edge and the cloud.

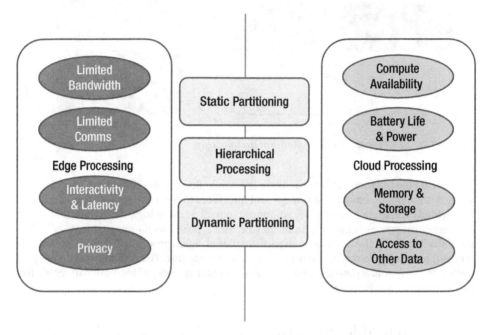

***Figure 7-2.*** *Example end-to-end system architectures*

A more detailed understanding of the platform architecture within the end-to-end system might be of interest as we explore the partitioning approach further. To accomplish this, we will explore five different platform examples: (a) simple sensor node, (b) wearable platform, (c) phone platform, (d) gateway platform, and (e) cloud server platform.

## 7.2.1    Sensor Node

A typical microcontroller-based sensor node architecture is shown in Figure 7-3. Such a platform typically has a microcontroller chip along with external sensors, a battery, and potentially an external communications chip as well. The growing trend is to integrate the communications functionality as part of the microcontroller SoC (system-on-chip).

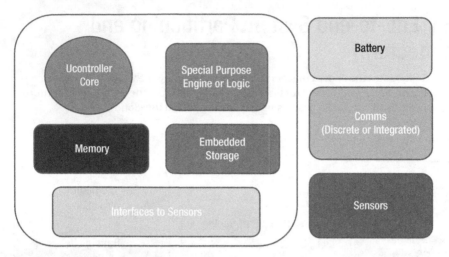

***Figure 7-3.*** *Example sensor node platform architecture*

Within the microcontroller SoC, there is a controller core for embedded processing along with memory, embedded storage, and interfaces to sensors. In addition to the embedded core, there is potentially additional special purpose logic or engines that enable sensor processing locally on the device. The type of special-purpose logic depends heavily on the usage but ranges from digital signal processing to security (crypto) processing to media processing to pattern matching. These platforms typically optimize for ultra-low power, especially leakage power, in order to increase battery life for predominantly inactive usages.

## 7.2.2 Wearable Platform

Another type of platform that is emerging and getting increasingly sophisticated is a wearable platform. A wearable platform architecture looks similar to the sensor node architecture, except that the core runs at higher frequencies. It is likely that there are two cores, one for higher performance while and the other for low power always-on processing. Such architectures also tend to have more special purpose logic for DSP (Digital Signal Processing), security, and other functionality. In addition, there is more communications and memory/storage capability in wearable platforms as compared to simplistic sensor nodes.

Figure 7-4 illustrates the key differences between a simplistic sensor platform and a wearable platform. A simplistic sensor node may primarily run bare-metal code written to it so one function executes extremely efficiently. Wearable platforms are getting more sophisticated and may run embedded operating systems to provide more rich functionality. Wearables may also have interfaces to displays, especially for devices like smart watches. While these displays are fairly small, they still provide a rich user interface for accessing different micro-applications and services for consumer usages.

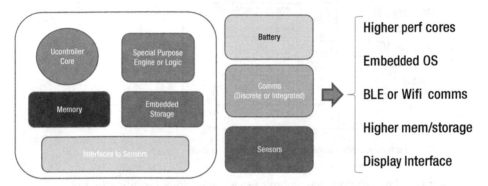

***Figure 7-4.*** *From sensor node to wearable platforms*

The key communications capabilities on wearable devices include Bluetooth and potentially Wi-Fi capabilities. Bluetooth provides the ability to build personal area networks within a short range. More recently, Bluetooth low energy (BLE) provides minimized Bluetooth communications but at ultra-low power and energy. Almost every operating system running on phone supports Bluetooth and BLE capabilities in order to enable connectivity to wearable platforms. By doing so, the phone can act as a more powerful hub for wearables as they get used on the go in daily life. Bluetooth provides special-purpose profiles ranging from health care to fitness to headset and beyond. Beyond Bluetooth, more powerful wearable platforms have recently started implementing Wi-Fi capabilities to provide more bandwidth in home environments but at the cost of additional power. Such capabilities are useful as wearable platforms include higher bandwidth sensors such as audio and video.

## 7.2.3   Phone Platform

The next major platform example is the phone platform. Today's phone platforms are very powerful, with multiple (potentially heterogeneous) cores, special purpose engines including graphics, connectivity capabilities, and significant memory and storage capabilities. Figure 7-5 shows an example of a mobile platform architecture that consists of the above key capabilities.

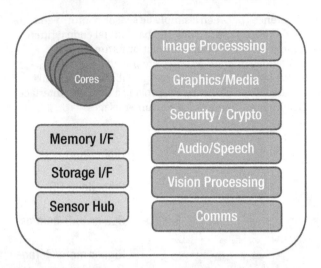

**Figure 7-5.** *Heterogeneous mobile platform architecture*

A smart phone platform has multiple usage dimensions, including: (a) rich visual experience with social media, video, and other playback capabilities, (b) rich communications experience with many cloud applications, (c) rich sensing capabilities with both external hard sensors, as well as soft sensing such as access to browsing, mail, and other user activities, and (d) rich application experience, with many available applications downloaded from a cloud store. In order to support all of these experiences, but within a form factor and battery life constraint, the architecture supports multiple levels of operation from always-on sensing to power-efficient light activity to high performance processing when required.

In order to support low-power execution, special purpose engines are developed and integrated into a phone platform for all of the important subsystems: (i) imaging, (ii) graphics and media processing, (iii) crypto processing, (iv) audio processing as well as speech recognition, (v) visual processing, and (vi) communications capabilities that include Bluetooth, Wi-Fi, and cellular subsystems. In addition, the phone platform also typically integrates a sensor hub to process rich sensor data from motion, location, audio, and vision at a low power profile. The smart phone platform has access to large memory and storage subsystems. In summary, a smart phone platform today is equivalent in compute capabilities to a small supercomputer from almost 25 years ago. This is especially evident when looking at the increasing core count in smart phone platforms and the continuous addition of memory and storage within the platform.

## 7.2.4   Gateway Platform

Our next platform description is for a gateway or hub platform. A gateway or hub platform has multiple processing cores, communications functionality that includes router capabilities along with media processing, and security as a key focus, especially if it is a hub platform or a set-top box in a home-like setting. In addition, it usually integrates a significant amount of memory and storage to handle a large amount of media, multiple simultaneous communication streams, and metadata storage. For set-top box-like capability, the ability to interface with digital cable as well as large displays becomes crucial and therefore the amount of processing, storage, and special purpose functionality increases further.

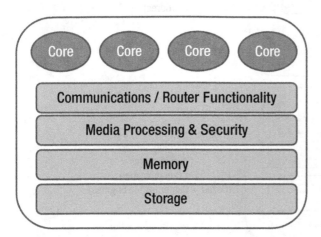

**Figure 7-6.** *Gateway or hub platform architecture*

Such a platform is typically not battery-operated (unlike devices discussed in this section previously) and therefore the gateway/hub is typically always wall-powered and available for processing at high performance. Employing such platforms as part of an end-to-end system architecture provides the opportunity to offload processing from the sensor/phone edge device to a central device like the gateway for both aggregation as well as high performance processing (saving battery power). At the same time, the gateway/hub can provide the benefits of low interactive latency since it is within the premise with high bandwidth communications capabilities like Wi-Fi.

## 7.2.5   Cloud Server Platform

Last but not least, we should also walk through the capabilities of a commercial server residing within a cloud datacenter. Traditionally, server platforms have a large number of cores (16-48 for example) and run at high performance, especially when it comes to throughput. Since multiple server platforms are in the cloud, the ability exists not only to do parallel processing within the server but also to accomplish parallel processing amongst multiple server machines within a cluster or within the overall datacenter. A simplistic description of a server platform architecture is shown in Figure 7-7 (top).

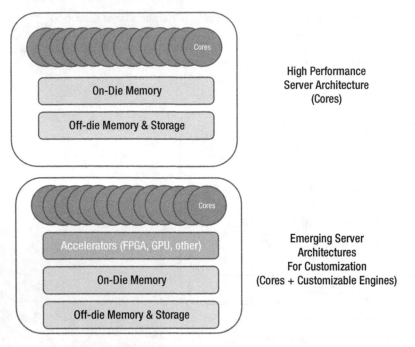

*Figure 7-7.* *Cloud server platform architectures*

More recent server architectures are attempting to provide customization for even high power-efficient performance. This includes the integration of programmable/reconfigurable logic like FPGAs (Field Programmable Gate Arrays) as well as other accelerators such as GPUs (Graphics Processor Units) and domain-specific engines.

As is probably evident in the picture in Figure 7-7, the abundance of high performance cores illustrates the higher compute capabilities of servers as compared to edge devices or gateways. Servers typically run within the power constraint of several 100 Watts as compared to phones which run at Watts and wearables or sensor nodes which are sub-Watt in battery life/capacity.

# 7.3   End-to-End Processing & Mapping Examples

The above description of each of the platforms hopefully illustrates the reason why an end-to-end system architecture is needed to accomplish a rich experience like visual recognition and processing. In order to delve into this further, let us consider three examples of processing: (a) speech processing, (b) visual processing, and (c) machine learning and classification tasks. These will further provide a current understanding of where certain tasks can be performed based on the considerations described earlier in this chapter. Let's start with speech processing.

## 7.3.1    Speech Processing Example

In order to understand speech processing in detail, let us consider an example usage. Consider a wearable device on the person's body that intends to provide the capability of an assistant who has the ability to answer questions. The end-to-end architecture for such a usage includes (a) wearable device on the body, (b) smart phone in the pocket, and (c) cloud platform in the datacenter. Here we recap the speech processing pipeline as well as the end-to-end system architecture in order to start considering how the partitioning could be accomplished between the different platforms listed above.

To recap the speech flow, a typical flow for Q&A assistance includes noise reduction (to clean the audio sample), voice activity detection (to detect human voice), keyword recognition (to identify the trigger word), speaker recognition (to identify the correct speaker), command and control (to identify commands), LVCSR (for continuous speech recognition), natural language processing (to determine what the words imply), and Q&A service (to determine the answer for the question).

For this example, the key considerations we will use to partition the speech flow on to the platforms in the end-to-end architecture are: (a) available compute within a constrained power and battery life envelope and (b) available memory capability for storing speech models needed for the processing. We will assume that other considerations are secondary in order to be able to illustrate implications of even just a few priorities.

Today, most devices only accomplish keyword recognition on an edge device like a wearable, smart phone, or even an ambient hub. But advances in low-power hardware designs are emerging to push the envelope on what can be processed closer to the edge rather than having to send all of the audio data to the cloud. These advances typically involve implementing speech algorithms using a hardware-software co-design approach. The resulting low power hardware design may not only be able to achieve keyword recognition but also some level of command & control (small vocabulary) on the local device at low power (milliwatts). As a result, a wearable in the near future should be able to provide processing for functionality all the way to limited command & control. Figure 7-8 shows an example partitioning of the speech pipeline over an end-to-end platform architecture.

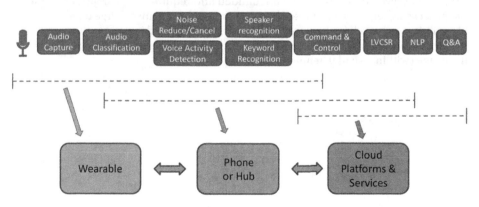

**Figure 7-8.** *End-to-end partitioning of speech flow (example)*

For a larger vocabulary in command & control but somewhat lower vocabulary in continuous speech recognition and natural language processing, a more powerful system in the end-to-end flow is required. With advances in HW/SW co-design, such capabilities should be possible on a smart phone or hub-like platform in the near future. Ultimately, for large-vocabulary speech recognition and full natural language processing, a cloud platform is needed not only to address the compute requirements but also to accommodate the memory needs for large and multiple language models. Last but not least, a question & answering service that is more generalized requires a cloud service since it requires public domain knowledge for determining appropriate answers based not only on the question but also on employing the context of the usage.

## 7.3.2   Visual Processing Example

Our next example of end-to-end partitioning (visual processing) considers a richer sensor (camera) and therefore more significant amounts of compute, bandwidth, and analytics. Here we consider the end-to-end architecture which considers a phone-like edge device (could also be a visual monitoring device with similar capabilities or even a mobile augmented reality device using a phone-like platform), a local hub that provides contextual data, and a cloud platform delivering richer visual services.

Figure 7-9 shows a few of the visual processing capabilities that are needed for most usages and a mapping of those to the potential platform where this can be achieved with compute, battery life, memory/storage capacity, and availability of contextual models and data in mind. We start with gesture recognition, which can be achieved locally. Gesture recognition can be recognition of hand poses as well as dynamic movements; and as long as the number of gestures are limited, the goal of recognition can be achieved on the edge device itself within 10s of milliwatts to 100s of milliwatts (based on complexity). As we start to consider object recognition, it gets more challenging for a local device to accomplish this, especially if the number of objects scale from 100s to 1000s to millions. For 100s of objects, a local device can provide the object models for object recognition and can achieve the recognition needed. However, if the objects are unbounded and require a large object database, the processing requires a cloud server that can match it against a large database. A hierarchical approach is also possible, where the local hub determines the context of the object recognition and caches some of the frequent objects that are expected in the usage (within a spatial/temporal distance).

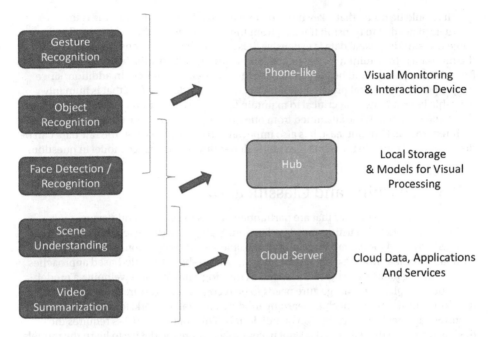

*Figure 7-9. Partitioning of visual processing (example)*

Similar to object recognition, processing for face recognition also depends on the number of faces involved (whether it is a home with a few faces vs. a corporation with 1000s of faces vs. a public query with millions of faces). Depending on this, the processing can be accomplished on the local edge device, the hub, or the cloud server. Face detection (knowing there is a face in the frame and identifying where it is) can certainly be accomplished on the local device, but face recognition requires a scalable hierarchical approach as described above.

Currently, there is a lot of research activity on scene understanding and video summarization. Understanding a scene implies knowing not only the individual entities in the image but also the activity or context in the scene. This requires each of the above capabilities (object, face, gesture) and more. Depending on the level of scene recognition required, it can be accomplished on the hub or in the cloud. Similarly, video summarization attempts to identify the salient scenes in a video and identify what the overall video consists of in terms of activity and storyline. Video summarization at a limited scale (identifying representative scenes that summarize the video) can be accomplished in the hub, whereas further summarization such as determining the activity and storyline may require cloud processing.

It should be noted that a key trade-off as we consider visual processing is the bandwidth needed to transmit the data from the local device to the hub to the cloud. Since transmitting visual data is expensive, it is also important to consider whether the raw data is transmitted from one node to the other, or if only the features extracted from the raw data should be transmitted for the processing required. In addition, since the purpose of the visual processing is not to create recorded content that is humanly viewable later, it is also not critical to maintain the highest resolution and frame rate for the visual stream as it is transmitted from one node to another in the end-to-end system architecture. Last but not least, it is also important to determine when the raw data can be discarded and only the metadata is retained depending on the usage model in question.

## 7.3.3 Learning and Classification

Another view of capabilities that are partitioned across the end-to-end system architecture is that of learning and classification. Machine learning techniques are increasingly used for pattern matching, audio, and visual recognition. The disruption with machine learning was that instead of writing code-based or rule-based approaches to recognizing patterns, actual data is used as training samples for developing a model.

For example, if an IMU gesture needs to be recognized, a gesture model can be developed by training a machine learning model (a neural network, for example) with gestures captured from a collection of individuals. This training process requires the device to capture the data but does not necessarily require the device to learn the models directly. A cloud-based solution can be used for training and development of the model and then the resulting model can be downloaded to the devices that are deployed in order to do the recognition during real-time.

Such partitioning can be thought of as two distinct steps: (a) offline training and (b) online classification. In fact, the base model used in many usages today relies on the cloud to do both offline training as well as online classification (as shown in Figure 7-10 top left). However, such a model has challenges when the latency to send raw data to the cloud for online classification becomes limiting to the usage. Therefore, newer models have emerged where the device does the classification by implementing the classification locally based on the trained model produced from the offline cloud training. Even this model can be restrictive when changes due to personalization or anomalies cannot be easily incorporated. As a result, researchers have been working on techniques for detecting anomalies and sending them to the cloud for updates to the local model. The cloud collects these anomalies and produces an updated model routinely and deploys the update to the field. Researchers are also trying to accomplish continuous learning by learning local changes on the device itself. These changes can not only be transmitted to the cloud for updates but also used to update the model locally.

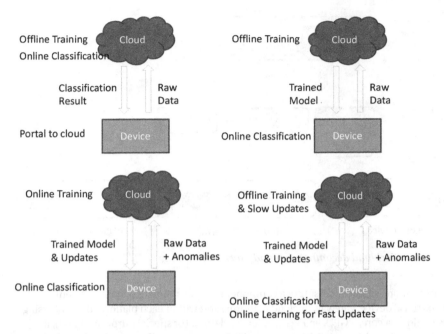

***Figure 7-10.*** *Learning and classification (offline vs. online)*

# 7.4   Programmability Considerations for End-to-End Partitioning

When implementing a sensing to knowledge management capability, it is also important to consider programmability of components of the solution. Since speech and visual algorithms are continuously evolving and variants of machine learning algorithms or neural networks are being developed every few months, it becomes critical that current implementations can be modified with ease. In addition, the previous sections in this chapter presented multiple partitioning possibilities and it becomes critical that these can also be dynamically changed if hardware or algorithm improvements become possible.

One approach is to develop APIs (application programming interfaces) that allow software developers to consistently use common interfaces but allow flexibility in modifying the implementation underneath. For example, if a speech pipeline employs HMMs (hidden Markov models) in their implementation for language models, changing this to WFST (weighted finite state transducers) in the future should be possible if the APIs are defined well and the implementation is flexible as a result.

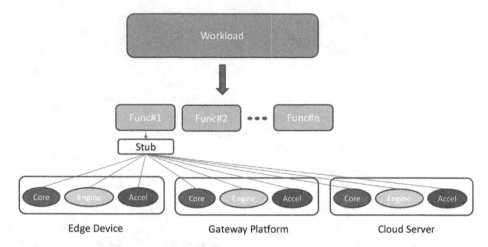

***Figure 7-11.*** *Workload decomposition and function mapping*

Furthermore, since processing of a component can be mapped to many different platforms (local device, gateway, or cloud platform) and within each platform the processing engine could be a core, a GPU, an FPGA, or an accelerator (or special purpose engine), it becomes important that the implementation abstracts these details to provide flexibility of changing the mapping and underlying components. An example of such a flexible approach is remote offloading where the authors propose an OpenCL-based solution for abstracting the function that needs to be executed such that it can be run on a local device or a remote platform and can also be run on any processing engine on these platforms (core or accelerator). Such solutions are gaining in popularity since heterogeneous architectures are becoming more common due to power/performance advantages. Figure 7-11 shows the decomposition of a workload into functional components and illustrates the use of a stub to redirect the execution of the function to any platform and processing engine within the platform. The policy used for determining where to run a function could be based on available bandwidth for data transfer, power/performance (affecting battery life of device), and potentially availability of the platform and engine (if multiple workloads are running simultaneously or the platform is not always available on the network).

# 7.5  Summary and Future Opportunities

This chapter presented the end-to-end architecture for sensor processing pipelines. As described in this chapter through various examples, there are multiple challenges in developing end-to-end system architectures for speech or vision capabilities and usages. This opens up many opportunities for further research and development. Here we will list a few of these opportunities:

- Developing special purpose engines and accelerators for specific algorithms and primitives

- Developing end-to-end system architectures that provide the ability for dynamic mapping and partitioning flexibility.

- Developing tools and models that allow for exploration of suitable partitioning policies

- Developing common processing pipelines across multiple usages

- Developing runtimes/programming models for end-to-end systems

## 7.6  Conclusion

This chapter concludes the overview of different facets of sensor data processing to make sense of the environments around us. We hope that the book achieved the goal of exposing the readers to a high-level understanding of the concepts and operations involved. The discussions in the book detailed the steps in making sense of sensors through (a) recognizing data from a single sensor, (b) using multiple sensing modes to improve recognition performance and implement new usages, (c) deriving usage context and in turn using the context for improving recognition operations, (d) deriving semantic relationships from recognized information, (e) representing the relationships to build knowledge graphs, (e) operating on the knowledge for implementing intelligent usages, and (d) system considerations for implementing sensor-driven knowledge pipelines.

While this book is aimed at providing a high-level bird's-eye view of the technologies involved, the content is aimed at providing a reader with an understanding of the generic nature of the knowledge pipeline across various sensing modes and usages. The information gained from the book should equip the reader with enough background to get to the next step of learning by choosing the domain and technology area of interest. The references provided at the end of the book chapters are a good start for such a quest.

## 7.7  References

- OpenCL: https://www.khronos.org/opencl/

- Eom, H., St Juste, P., Figueiredo, R., Tickoo, O., Illikkal, R. and R. Iyer. "OpenCL-based Remote Offloading Framework for Trusted Mobile Cloud Computing." IEEE International Conference on Parallel and Distributed Systems (ICPADS '13).

- Iyer, R., Srinivasan, S., Tickoo, O., Fang, Z., Illikkal, R., Zhang, S., Chadha, V., Stillwell, Jr., P. M. and S. E. Lee. "CogniServe: Heterogeneous Server Architecture for Large-Scale Recognition." *IEEE Micro* 31, no. 3 (2011): 20–31,

- Barroso, L.A., Dean, J. and U. Holzle. "Web Search for a Planet: The Google Cluster Architecture." *IEEE Micro* 23, no. 2 (2003): 22–28.

- Takacs, G. et al. "Outdoors Augmented Reality on Mobile Phone Using Loxel-Based Visual Feature Organization." *Proc. ACM 1st Int'l Conf. Multimedia Information Retrieval (MIR 08)*, (2008): 427–434.

- Bay, H. et al. "Speeded-Up Robust Features (SURF)." *J. Computer Vision and Image Understanding* 110, no. 3 (200): 346–359.

- Lowe, D.G. "Distinctive Image Features from Scale-Invariant Keypoints." *Int'l J. Computer Vision* 60, no. 2 (2004): 91–110.

- Srinivasan, S. et al. "Performance Characterization and Acceleration of Optical Character Recognition on Handheld Platforms." *Proc. IEEE Int'l Symp. Workload Characterization (IISWC 10)* (2010).

- Andersen, D.G. et al. "FAWN: A Fast Array of Wimpy Nodes." *Proc. ACM SIGOPS 22nd Symp. Operating Systems Principles (SOSP 09)* (2009): 1–14.

- V. Reddi et al., "Web Search Using Mobile Cores: Quantifying and Mitigating the Price of Efficiency," Proc. 37th Ann. Int'l Symp. Computer Architecture (ISCA 10), ACM Press, 2010, pp. 314–325.

# Index

# Get the eBook for only $4.99!

Why limit yourself?

Now you can take the weightless companion with you wherever you go and access your content on your PC, phone, tablet, or reader.

Since you've purchased this print book, we are happy to offer you the eBook for just $4.99.

Convenient and fully searchable, the PDF version enables you to easily find and copy code—or perform examples by quickly toggling between instructions and applications.

To learn more, go to http://www.apress.com/us/shop/companion or contact support@apress.com.